JUDAISM AND HEALING

HALAKHIC PERSPECTIVES

JUDAISM
AND
HEALING

HALAKHIC PERSPECTIVES

by

J. DAVID BLEICH

KTAV PUBLISHING HOUSE, INC.

Library of Congress Cataloging in Publication Data
Bleich, J David.
Judaism and healing.

Bibliography: p.
Includes index.
1. Medical laws and legislation (Jewish law)
2. Medicine and Judaism. 3. Medical ethics.
I. Title.
Law 296.1'8 80-26441
ISBN 0-87068-891-X
ISBN 0-87068-289-X (pbk.)

MANUFACTURED IN THE UNITED STATES OF AMERICA

Table of Contents

אמר הקב״ה אין מכה שאין לה רפואה ונכרת רפואתה וסמה של כל מכה ומכה אם מבקש את שלא יגיע לגופך צרה עסוק בתורה שהיא רפואה לכל הגוף.

תנחומא יתרו ח׳

Said the Holy One, blessed be He: "There is no affliction for which there does not exist a cure; the therapy and medicament for every affliction is discernible. If you seek that misfortune befall not your body engage in the study of Torah, for it is a therapy for the entire body."

Tanchuma, Yitro 8

Preface

This volume is an expanded version of a study prepared under a grant to the Agudath Israel of America by the National Endowment for the Humanities as part of its ethnic heritage program. The material is designed to present in a non-technical manner the values and teachings of the Judaic tradition as brought to bear upon contemporary issues in bioethics.

I am indebted to Dr. David Singer for his encouragement and assistance in my initial undertaking of this nature, a course syllabus on behalf of the University Without Walls under the sponsorship of Haifa University and the American Jewish Committee. I also wish to express appreciation to my brother-in-law, Rabbi Mordecai Ochs, for his painstaking reading of the manuscript and for his many helpful suggestions; to my good friend, Dr. Fred Rosner, for continually drawing my attention to items of ethical and halakhic concern which appear in the medical literature; to Drs. David Horowitz and Richard Lopchinsky for making their knowledge and expertise readily available to me; and *le-talmidai yoter mi-kullam,* to the students of the *Chaver* Program at *Yeshivat Rabbenu Yitzchak Elchanan* and to the participants in my seminar in Medicine and Halakhah at the Albert Einstein College of Medicine whose insightful questions have spurred my ongoing investigations in medical halakhah.

Introduction

The rapid developments which have occurred in medicine and the biological sciences in recent years have brought in their wake a host of moral and ethical problems. Although the issues are not necessarily new, they present themselves with increasing frequency and in contexts which make the seeking of resolutions a matter of high priority. This has resulted in the emergence of what is fast becoming a new academic discipline—bioethics—an interdisciplinary investigation involving specialists in the diverse fields of philosophy, theology, medicine, law, and science, in efforts to formulate answers to the questions which are now being raised.

Judaism, as a system of law and ethics, has much to say with regard to these issues. Jewish tradition is rich in sources bearing upon the formulation of bioethical perspectives. This monograph is designed to acquaint the reader with the viewpoint of Judaism as it relates to the problems of bioethics.

The subject matter of this book ranges over many areas of thought. Questions pertaining to bioethics affect the life, the health, and, ultimately, the moral condition of each and every member of society. The problems under discussion are not merely of abstract theoretical interest; they are of immediate importance and applicability. The reader is here afforded a fascinating study in the practical application of fundamental concepts of Jewish thought to the day-by-day realities of modern life. Jewish bioethics represents the merging of theory and practice. It is a discipline in which abstractions become concrete and in which Judaism offers unique answers to ethical dilemmas of contemporary life.

Jews, to whom all such questions are quests not simply for

applicable utilitarian principles, but for divine guidance, must, of necessity, seek answers in the teachings of the Torah. "The Torah of God is perfect" (Psalms 19:8), and in its teachings the discerning student will find eternally valid answers to even newly-formulated queries. As physicians and patients turn to rabbinic authorities for answers, Jewish scholars seek to elucidate and expound the teachings of the Torah in these vital areas of concern.

The discussions which follow draw primarily upon talmudic sources, rulings incorporated in the various codes of Jewish law, and subsequent responsa literature. This is so because Judaism is fundamentally a religion of law. Halakhah (religious law) governs virtually every facet of human endeavor. An individual who seeks to find answers within the Jewish tradition can deal with such questions in only one way. He must examine them through the prism of Halakhah, for it is in the corpus of Jewish law as elucidated and transmitted from generation to generation that God has made His will known to man.

The source of Halakhah is, of course, divine revelation. To the basic corpus of biblical law were added rabbinic enactments and decrees. Biblical law is, however, not limited to material explicitly recorded in Scripture. Judaism regards both the Oral and Written Law as the product of revelation. Jewish tradition teaches that Moses received on Mount Sinai not only the Pentateuch (the Five Books of Moses), which was committed to writing, but also a much more lengthy and detailed corpus of law supplementing the Written Law. The latter was transmitted orally from generation to generation until it was subsequently recorded in the Mishnah and amplified in the Gemara. The Mishnah and the Gemara are together referred to as the Talmud, which serves as the primary source of the formulation of Halakhah. It is for this reason that virtually all halakhic determinations are ultimately grounded on talmudic citations.

Since the Talmud is voluminous and contains analysis, discussion, and commentary, as well as matters entirely extraneous to Halakhah, the need arose for concise compendia which would contain definitive, but succinct rulings. The most frequently cited of these codes of law are Maimonides' *Mishneh Torah* (12th cent.) and the *Shulchan Arukh* authored by Rabbi Joseph Karo (16th cent.).

At times there are ambiguities in the texts. Sometimes, later scholars disagreed with the conclusions reached by the authors of these codes. As a result, during the course of centuries a large number of commentaries to these codes were composed. Moreover, as might be expected, these codes could not possibly contain rulings for every conceivable question which might arise. This gave rise to a vast responsa literature or "case law." Questions were addressed to individual rabbinic scholars who frequently wrote lengthy responsa detailing the sources and reasoning upon which their answers were based. All of this material, from the Mishnah until the most recent responsa works, constitutes the halakhic corpus from which rabbinic teaching on any matter of Jewish law must be derived.

The material presented in each of the following chapters is culled from these classical sources, and is designed to acquaint the reader with the teachings of Judaism with regard to topical issues in bioethics. An attempt has been made to discuss these complex topics in as non-technical a manner as possible. Of necessity, comprehensive analysis has been sacrificed in order to achieve this goal. If the interest of the reader is awakened and he or she is prompted to seek further information, the author will deem his efforts to have been amply rewarded.

The author is keenly aware of the potential dangers and pitfalls attendant upon compilation of a précis of halakhic material. Such considerations assume even greater proportions when the presentation is in the vernacular. Yet, particularly in areas which are the subject of discussion on the part of society in general, failure to articulate the teachings of Judaism in a readily understandable manner inevitably leads to misconstrual of Jewish law. On balance, the dangers of silence are graver than those of publication. Halakhic authorities of earlier generations repeatedly warned that one should not attempt to glean definitive answers to specific questions from halakhic handbooks and compendia. That cautionary admonition applies, *a fortiori,* to a work such as this. The final adjudication of any particular question hinges upon any number of variables. Accordingly, in any particular instance the reader is urged to present all pertinent details to a competent rabbinic authority for determination of the halakhic ruling on a case-by-case basis.

1

The Obligation to Heal

Judaism teaches that the value of human life is supreme and takes precedence over virtually all other considerations. This attitude is most eloquently summed up in a talmudic passage regarding the creation of Adam: "Therefore only a single human being was created in the world, to teach that if any person has caused a single soul of Israel to perish, Scripture regards him as if he had caused an entire world to perish; and if any human being saves a single soul of Israel, Scripture regards him as if he had saved an entire world" (*Sanhedrin* 37a). Human life is not a good to be preserved as a condition of other values but an absolute, basic, and precious good in its own right. The obligation to preserve life is commensurately all-encompassing.

The obligation to save the life of an endangered person is derived by the Talmud, *Sanhedrin* 73a, from the verse "Nor shall you stand idly by the blood of your fellow" (Leviticus 19:16). The Talmud and the various codes of Jewish law offer specific examples of situations in which a moral obligation exists with regard to rendering aid. These include the rescue of a person drowning in a river, assistance to one being mauled by wild beasts, and aid to a person under attack by bandits.

The application of this principle to medical intervention for the purposes of preserving life is not without theological and philosophical difficulties. It is to be anticipated that a theology which ascribes providential concern to the Deity will view sickness as part of the divine scheme. A personal God does not allow His creatures, over whom He exercises providential guardianship, to become ill unless the affliction is divinely ordained as a means of punishment, for purposes of expiation of sin, or for some other beneficial purpose entirely comprehensible to the Deity, if not to man.

Human intervention in causing or speeding the therapeutic process is, then, in a sense, interference with the deliberate design of providence. It would then appear that the patient, in seeking medical attention, betrays a lack of faith in failing to put his trust in God. The Karaites rejected all forms of human healing and relied entirely upon prayer. Consistent with their fundamentalist orientation, they based their position upon a quite literal reading of Exodus 15:26. A literal translation of the Hebrew text of the passage reads as follows: "I will put none of the diseases upon you which I have put upon the Egyptians, for I am the Lord your physician."[1] Hence the Karaites taught that God alone should be sought as physician.

This view was rejected by Judaism, but not without due recognition of the cogency of the theological argument upon which it is based. Rabbinic teaching recognized that intervention for the purpose of thwarting the natural course of the disease could be sanctioned only on the basis of specific divine dispensation. Such license is found, on the basis of talmudic exegesis, in the scriptural passage dealing with compensation for personal injury:

> And if men quarrel with one another and one smites the other with a stone or with the fist and he die not, but has to keep in bed . . . he must pay the loss entailed by absence from work and he shall cause him to be thoroughly healed. (Exodus 21:19–20)

Ostensibly, this passage refers simply to financial liability incurred as the result of an act of assault. However, since specific reference is made to liability for medical expenses, it follows that liability for such expenses implies biblical license to incur those expenses in the course of seeking the ministrations of a practitioner of the healing arts. Thus the Talmud, *Baba Kamma* 85a, comments, "From here [it is derived] that the physician is granted permission to cure." Specific authorization is required, comments Rashi, in order to teach us that ". . . we are not to say, 'How is it that God smites and man heals?' " In much the same vein, *Tosafot* and R. Solomon ben Abraham

Aderet state that, without such sanction, "He who heals might appear as if he has invalidated a divine decree."

Non-therapeutic life-saving intervention is talmudically mandated on independent grounds. The Talmud, *Sanhedrin* 73a, posits an obligation to rescue a neighbor from danger, such as drowning or being mauled by an animal. This obligation is predicated upon the scriptural exhortation with regard to the restoration of lost property, "And you shall restore it to him" (Deuteronomy 22:2). On the basis of a pleonasm in the Hebrew text, the Talmud declares that this verse includes an obligation to restore a fellow-man's body as well as his property. Hence, there is created an obligation to come to the aid of one's fellow-man in a life-threatening situation.[2] Noteworthy is the fact that Maimonides,[3] going beyond the examples supplied by the Talmud, posits this source as the basis of the obligation to render medical care. Maimonides declares that the biblical commandment "And you shall restore it to him" establishes an obligation requiring the physician to render professional services in life-threatening situations. Every individual, insofar as he is able, is obligated to restore the health of a fellow-man no less than he is obligated to restore his property. Maimonides views this as a binding religious obligation.

Noteworthy is not only Maimonides' extension of this concept to cover medical matters but also his failure to allude at all to the verse "And he shall cause him to be thoroughly healed." It would appear that Maimonides is of the opinion that without the granting of specific *permission* one would not be permitted to tamper with physiological processes; obligations derived from Deuteronomy 22:2 would be limited to prevention of accident or assault by man or beast. Dispensation to intervene in the natural order is derived from Exodus 21:20; but once such license is given, medical therapy is not simply elective but acquires the status of a positive obligation.[4]

As indicated by *Sanhedrin* 73a, this obligation mandates not only the rendering of personal assistance, as is the case with regard to the restoration of lost property, but, by virtue of the negative commandment, "Nor shall you stand idly by the blood of your fellow" (Leviticus 19:16), the obligation is expanded to encompass expenditure of financial resources for the sake of preserving the life of one's fellow-man. This seems to have been the interpretation given to Maimonides' comments by Rabbi Joseph Karo, who, in his code of Jewish law, *Yoreh De'ah* 336:1, combined both concepts in stating:

> The Torah gave permission to the physician to heal; moreover, this is a religious precept and is included in the category of saving life; and if the physician withholds his services it is considered as shedding blood.[5]

Nachmanides also finds that the obligation of the physician to heal is inherent in the commandment "And you shall love your neighbor as yourself" (Leviticus 19:18).[6] As a specific instance of the general obligation to manifest love and concern for one's neighbor, the obligation to heal encompasses not only situations posing a threat to life or limb or demanding restoration of impaired health, but also situations of lesser gravity warranting medical attention for relief of pain and promotion of well-being.

A latter-day authority, R. Yehudah Leib Zirelson, in his *Teshuvot Atzei ha-Levanon,* no. 61, argues cogently that the obligations posited by the Gemara, *Sanhedrin* 73a, apply under non-life-threatening circumstances no less than in life-threatening situations. The verse "And you shall restore it to him" (Deuteronomy 22:2) mandates not only the return of lost property but, *a fortiori,* preservation of life as well. The verse, then, does not refer only to the return of objects of material value. Accordingly, declares *Atzei ha-Levanon,* restoration of health to a person suffering from an illness is assuredly included in the commandment "And you shall restore it to him."

Atzei ha-Levanon further demonstrates that failure to provide a medical remedy, when available, entails violation both of the commandment "You may not hide yourself" (Deuteronomy 22:3), which, in its biblical context, refers to a person who comes upon lost property belonging to another, and the admonition "Nor shall you stand idly by the blood of your fellow" (Leviticus 19:16). *Sifra, Kedoshim* 41, declares that these commandments establish an obligation making it incumbent upon an individual to act, if he is capable of doing so, in order to prevent his fellow from sustaining a financial loss. This obligation is recorded by Rambam, *Hilkhot Rotzeach* 1:13; *Sefer ha-*

Chinnukh, no. 237; and *Shulchan Arukh, Choshen Mishpat* 426:1. It similarly follows that a person is bound by the same commandments to prevent loss or deterioration of health if he possesses the requisite knowledge and skill to be of assistance in providing medical care. Failure to do so, concludes *Atzei ha-Levanon,* would constitute transgression of these two negative commandments as well as of the positive commandment "And you shall restore it to him." Furthermore, as noted earlier, according to Nachmanides, failure to render medical assistance entails abrogation of the positive commandment "And you shall love your neighbor as yourself." Thus, even in situations which pose no threat to life, a person in a position to do so is bound by no less than four separate *mitzvot* to render medical assistance.

Despite the unequivocal and authoritative rulings of both Maimonides and Rabbi Joseph Karo, there do exist within the rabbinic tradition dissonant views which look somewhat askance at the practice of the healing arts. Abraham ibn Ezra (*Commentary on the Bible,* Exodus 21:19) finds a contradiction between the injunction "And he shall cause to be thoroughly healed," and the account given in II Chronicles 16:12. Scripture reports that Asa, King of Judah, became severely ill and, in his sickness, "he sought not to the Lord, but to the physicians." Of course, this passage can readily be understood as implying that Asa was deserving of censure because he relied upon mortal physicians exclusively and failed to seek divine help through penitence and prayer. If the verse in question is interpreted in this light, it contains no disparaging reference whatsoever with regard to either physicians or to the practice of medicine. Rabbinic scholars, including exegetes such as *Metzudat David* and legal authorities such as R. Joel Sirkes, *Bayit Chadash, Yoreh De'ah* 336, do indeed interpret this passage in precisely this way. Alternatively, the passage may be understood as censuring Asa for not recognizing that the physician and his ministrations are merely vehicles for divine healing and that all healing ultimately comes from God.[7]

However, Ibn Ezra, and later Nachmanides as well, understood this verse as teaching that Asa was censured for seeking medical assistance. According to Ibn Ezra, Asa was taken to task for not placing his trust in God alone[8] to the exclusion of endeavors to effect a cure through the vehicle of medical science. Seen in this light, there is a clear contradiction between II Chronicles 16:12 and Exodus 21:19. Ibn Ezra resolves this difficulty by examining the contextual reference of each passage. Exodus refers to an act of physical assault. The healing to which specific reference is made is treatment of a presumably external wound which is humanly inflicted. II Chronicles speaks of sickness undoubtedly resulting from "natural" physiological processes. According to Ibn Ezra, Scripture grants license for therapeutic intervention only for treatment of external wounds. Wounds inflicted by man, either by design or by accident, may legitimately be treated by any means known to mankind. That which has been inflicted by man may be cured by man. However, internal wounds or physiological disorders, according to this view, are not encompassed in the injunction "and he shall cause to be thoroughly healed." Such afflictions are presumed to be manifestations of divine rebuke or punishment, and only God, who afflicts, may heal.

Needless to say, Ibn Ezra's position was rejected by normative Judaism, as is most eloquently demonstrated by the ruling recorded in *Shulchan Arukh, Orach Chaim* 328:3. Jewish law not only sanctions but requires suspension of Sabbath restrictions for treatment of a person afflicted by a life-threatening malady. In a blanket ruling, *Orach Chaim* 328:3 declares that all internal wounds are to be presumed to be life-threatening for purposes of Halakhah. Quite obviously, Jewish law, as codified, mandates treatment of even internal disorders by means of all available therapeutic techniques.

Nevertheless, permission to seek medical intervention is perceived as a concession to man's perceived needs. Ideally, were man to exist in a state of spiritual perfection, he would be bidden to rely entirely upon God's providence. Nachmanides, in his commentary on Leviticus 26:11, states clearly that when Israel achieved a state of spiritual perfection in the period of the Prophets, people turned to the Prophets when they fell ill rather than to the physicians. "What portion is there unto physicians in the house of those who do the will of God, since He has vouchsafed, 'and He will bless your bread and your water and I will remove sickness from your midst'?"

Reliance upon the will of God exclusively is possible only in a spiritual utopia. In developing his theory of providence,

Maimonides (*Guide of the Perplexed,* III, chaps. 17–18) explains that the quality of providential guardianship extended to man is directly correlative with man's spiritual attainment. To the extent that man is lacking in perfection his condition is regulated by the laws of nature. Thus, a pious person privileged to be the recipient of a high degree of providential guardianship would not require medication, but might expect to be healed by God directly. Other individuals, not beneficiaries of this degree of providence, are perforce required to seek a cure by natural means. In doing so they incur no censure whatsoever. Indeed, Nachmanides prefaces his comments with a reference to such times when the people of "Israel are perfect" and specifically states that failure to seek medical attention was normative only "for the righteous," and even for them solely "during the time of prophecy." Lesser individuals living in spiritually imperfect epochs are duty-bound to seek the cures made available by medical science. In terms of normative Jewish law, there is no question that there exists a positive obligation to seek medical care.[9]

An eloquent midrashic narrative reflects both recognition of man's inherent lack of authority to tamper with physiological processes, since, *prima facie,* such intervention could be construed as a violation of the natural order, as well as awareness that permission to practice the medical arts is a matter of specific divine dispensation:

> It occurred that R. Ishmael and R. Akiva were strolling in the streets of Jerusalem accompanied by another person. They were met by a sick person. He said to them, "My masters, tell me by what means I may be cured." They told him, "Do thus and so until you are cured." [The sick man] asked them, "And who afflicted me?" They replied, "The Holy One, blessed by He." [The sick man] responded, "You have entered into a matter which does not pertain to you. [God] has afflicted and you seek to cure! Are you not transgressing His will?"
>
> [R. Akiva and R. Ishmael] asked him, "What is your occupation?" [The sick man] answered, "I am a tiller of the soil and here is the sickle in my hand." They asked him, "Who created the vineyard?" He answered, "The Holy One, blessed be He." R. Akiva and R. Ishmael said to him, "And you enter into a matter which does not pertain to you! [God] created [the vineyard] and you cut

> His fruits from it." He said to them, "Do you not see the sickle in my hand? If I did not plow, sow, fertilize, and weed, nothing would sprout." [R. Akiva and R. Ishmael] said to him, "Foolish man! Have you never in your life heard that it is written, 'as for man, his days are as grass; as a flower of the field, so he flourishes' (Psalms 103:15). Just as if one does not weed, fertilize, and plow, the trees will not produce [fruit], and if fruit is produced but is not watered or fertilized it will not live but die, so with regard to the body. Drugs and medicaments are the fertilizer and the physician is the tiller of the soil."[10]

The analogy between the physician and the farmer is drawn with the utmost precision. Prior to the flood man was forbidden to eat the flesh of animals. Only after Noah emerged from the Ark did God tell Noah, "Every moving thing which lives shall be food for you; as the green herb have I given you all" (Genesis 9:3). The Gemara, *Sanhedrin* 59b, points out that Adam was not permitted to eat meat but was restricted to the produce of the field. Permission to eat growing things is granted to Adam in the verse "And God said: 'Behold, I have given you every herb yielding seed which is upon the face of all the earth and every tree . . . to you it shall be for food" (Genesis 1:29). In the absence of this dispensation Adam would have been forbidden to partake in any way of the bounty of the Garden of Eden. Any attempt on his part to do so would have been an act of theft.

Before Adam sinned it was not necessary for him to till the soil. "With the sweat of your face shall you eat bread" (Genesis 3:19) is indeed a curse, but it is a dispensation as well. Without such dispensation Adam would have had no right to plow the field or to uproot thorns and thistles. One who enters his neighbor's field and engages in such acts is an intruder and usurper. Since the land was created by God, Adam had no right to till the soil unless given specific dispensation. In declaring "By the sweat of your brow shall you eat bread" God at one and the same time grants permission to till the soil and indicates that henceforth it is the divine will that Adam do so. Adam may no longer simply rely only upon the largesse of God; he *must* till the soil for sustenance.

The analogy drawn by the Midrash is an obvious one. The sick man viewed therapeutic intervention as a contravention of the divine will, and application of medicaments as illicit interference with the natural processes of the human body, which is the chattel of God. Indeed this is so, but, by the same token, fields and vineyards are the property of God as well, and man has no natural right to till the soil or to pluck the fruits which the land produces. Man may do so, not as a matter of right, but by virtue of specific divine dispensation. Man is similarly granted dispensation to practice the medical arts. Just as God grants permission to till the soil and to reap the harvest in order that man shall not perish, so also does He grant dispensation to seek medical assistance in order to restore the body to health.

It is clear, then, that in the absence of specific scriptural license to practice the healing arts, Jews would be forbidden to seek the therapeutic benefits of medical science. Accordingly, despite the serious nature of the halakhic imperative with regard to the preservation of life and health, it is not surprising that this imperative is somewhat circumscribed insofar as the practice of medicine is concerned. The limitations, few as they are, serve as a reminder that all healing comes from God.

NOTES

1. See Abraham Ibn Ezra, *Commentary on the Bible,* Exodus 15:26.

2. Nachmanides, in his commentary on the verse "and your brother shall live with you" (Leviticus 25:35), declares that this verse is to be understood as a commandment establishing a general obligation to save the life of one's fellow.

3. *Commentary on the Mishnah, Nedarim* 4:4. Cf. *Mishneh Torah, Hilkhot Nedarim* 6:8.

4. Cf. R. Baruch ha-Levi Epstein, *Torah Temimah,* Exodus 21:19 and Deuteronomy 22:2.

5. See also R. Eliezer Waldenberg, *Ramat Rachel,* no. 10, and idem, *Tzitz Eli'ezer,* X, no. 25, chap. 7.

6. *Torat ha-Adam* in *Kitvei Ramban,* ed. Bernard Chavel (Jerusalem, 5724), II, 48.

7. See R. Solomon ben Abraham Aderet, *Teshuvot ha-Rashba,* I, no. 413.

8. Cf. Bachya ibn Pakuda, *Chovot ha-Levavot, Sha'ar ha-Bitachon,* chap. 3.

9. See Bachya ibn Pakuda, *Chovot ha-Levavot, Sha'ar ha-Bitachon,* chap. 4; *Besamim Rosh,* no. 386; R. Simon ben Zemach Duran, *Teshuvot Tashbatz,* III, no. 82; R. Joel Sirkes, *Bayit Chadash, Yoreh De'ah*

336; R. Abraham Gumbiner, *Magen Avraham, Orach Chaim* 328:6; R. Chaim Yosef David Azulai, *Birkei Yosef, Yoreh De'ah* 336:2; R. Moses Sofer, *Teshuvot Chatam Sofer, Orach Chaim,* no. 176; R. Ya'akov Ettlinger, *Binyan Zion,* no. 111; R. Samson Morpug, *Shemesh Tzedakah, Yoreh De'ah,* no. 29; R. Moses ben Abraham Mat, *Matteh Mosheh,* IV, chap. 3; R. Nissim Abraham Ashkenazi, *Ma'aseh Avraham, Yoreh De'ah,* no. 55; R. Nathan Nate Landau, *Kenaf Renanah, Orach Chaim,* no. 60; R. Yehudah Eyush, *Shivtei Yehudah,* no. 336; R. Ya'akov Prager, *She'ilat Ya'akov,* no. 5; R. Israel Meir ha-Kohen, *Mishnah Berurah, Orach Chaim* 328:6; R. Ovadiah Yosef, *Yabia Omer,* IV, *Choshen Mishpat,* no. 6, sec. 4; R. Eliezer Waldenberg, *Ramat Rachel,* no. 20; idem., *Tzitz Eli'ezer,* IX, no. 17, chap. 6, sec. 17; X, no. 25, chaps. 19 and 20; and XI, no. 41; and R. Joshua Neuwirth, *Shemirat Shabbat ke-Hilkhatah* 19:2.

10. *Midrash Temurah,* ed. J. D. Eisenstein, *Otzar Midrashim* (New York, 1915), II, 580–581.

2

The Role of the Physician

Judaism, as we have seen, views the seeking of medical attention as a moral imperative. Moreover, man is obligated to exercise prudence in perserving health. Thus the Talmud, *Sanhedrin* 17b, states that a scholar should not establish residence in a community which cannot boast of the presence of a physician.

Despite the obligation on the part of the patient to seek medical care, the concomitant obligation on the part of the physician is somewhat limited. There is no absolute, mandatory obligation which requires any specific individual to study medicine, no matter how talented he may be.[1] Similarly, no person is obligated to engage in any specific research designed to advance medical knowledge. By the same token, even after having received extensive medical training and having been licensed to practice medicine, no individual is obligated to enter into the practice of medicine as a vocation or to seek out patients in need of his professional skill and expertise.

However, if a physician is requested to render medical assistance, or if the physician becomes aware of the needs of an individual requiring medical assistance, the situation is quite different. The legal system of our country is firmly rooted in Anglo-Saxon common law. Under that legal system the relationship between a physician and his patient is a contractual one. Therefore, legally, a doctor has the absolute right to refuse to treat a patient who is not yet under his care. In effect, he may refuse to enter into a contract with the would-be patient. This attitude is reflected in the Code of Ethics of the American Medical Association, which declares, "A physician may choose whom he will serve." Judaism, to the contrary, regards the physician not simply as acting on behalf of the patient but as acting in the service of God. He is, in effect, God's messenger and dares not shirk the responsibility thrust upon him. This, quite apart from a general aversion to oath-taking, serves to explain why there is absent in the Jewish tradition any parallel to the Hippocratic Oath. Judaism has no knowledge of "ceremonial" oaths. No official swears an oath to discharge his duties faithfully. Witnesses are not "sworn in" in Jewish courts of law. Jews are considered to be "foresworn from Sinai" to observe all the tenets of Judaism. For one who has sworn at Sinai to observe the tenets of Judaism in their entirety, a subsequent oath to fulfill any specific religious obligation would be superfluous.

Accordingly, the doctor is under halakhic obligation to render medical care not only in emergency, life-threatening situations but even when such care is required simply for alleviation of pain or preservation of physical well-being. Man intuitively perceives a social morality which leads to the recognition that man *is* his brother's keeper. Men feel themselves to be reciprocally obligated to preserve the life, safety, and well-being of fellow members of the human community. Human society has long recognized that unique obligations devolve upon certain of its members by virtue of their talents, training, and/or unique responsibilities. A swimmer who blithely ignores the plight of a drowning person acts in a morally reprehensible manner. "Nor shall you stand idly by the blood of your fellow" (Leviticus 19:16) is the scriptural formulation of the ethical imperative which mandates life-saving intervention. Not all men share equally in this responsibility. Obviously, a non-swimmer cannot be required to plunge into dangerous waters; his efforts would be futile at best. But, in a life-threatening situation, surely a skilled swimmer is morally bound to place himself at the disposal of his fellow-man. Enhancement of skills brings in its wake a commensurate increase in moral responsibility.

It is instructive to compare the obligations of the physician with those of the Torah scholar who is requested to impart information or to serve as an arbiter or judge in civil disputes. One of the foremost nineteenth-century rabbinic authorities, R.

Moses Sofer, *Teshuvot Chatam Sofer, Choshen Mishpat,* no. 164, indicates that, as a matter of strict obligation, the scholar need not seek out persons in need of his services, nor must he make himself available during such times as he is engaged in earning a livelihood. But, when engaged in study, or in his free time, he must answer questions put to him and render decisions "for with regard to this, that which concerns his fellow-man takes precedence." The physician, in situations in which the life of his fellow-man may be threatened, labors under an even greater obligation. When able to do so, he must act in order to preserve human life.

An individual physician might, indeed, sidestep his responsibilities by removing himself from situations in which his aid might be sought. While such conduct, to be sure, would not merit approbation, the physician who acts in this manner would not incure the guilt of a technical halakhic infraction.

Society, however, has wider responsibilities which are accompanied by broad-ranging authority. Within autonomous Jewish communities, society's responsibility for promotion of communal well-being is discharged through the *Bet Din* (rabbinical court). Thus, the *Bet Din* is empowered to compel the physician to make himself available and to function in his professional capacity. Furthermore, it is the responsibility of the *Bet Din* to assure that the burden of providing medical care is shared equitably by all physicians qualified to render such care.[2]

These statements reflect the view that diverse obligations devolve upon the individual and upon society. The obligations of society are not only greater but are qualitatively different. An individual must respond to an immediate danger. While every individual aware of the danger and capable of alleviating that danger is obligated to respond, such individuals, no matter how large their number may be, respond as individuals rather than as members of a society. Yet no person is obligated to prepare himself to respond to an as yet non-existent danger. The individual's responsibility to act is limited to a danger which is clear and imminent.

Moral responsibility is readily perceived in the context of direct, proximate, causal relationships. Obligations in less proximate situations are not at all obvious. For example, is a person obligated to develop life-saving skills so that he can succor others in time of need? Certainly, acquisition of such skills should be encouraged and is surely deserving of approbation. But is it incumbent upon any given individual to acquire such skills?

Society as a whole may well be obligated to train lifeguards and to post them at public beaches, but no individual need necessarily feel obligated to make this profession his life vocation. The training and deployment of policemen, firemen, lifeguards, etc., in anticipation of potential emergencies, is a societal rather than a personal obligation. But, subsequent to completion of training and acceptance of responsibility, the members of these professions do assume personal obligations.

A similar distinction may be employed in resolving dilemmas arising fron conflicting moral duties. May a person on his way to a class in first-aid instruction ignore the plight of a dying man on the plea that he must perfect skills which may enable him to rescue a greater number of persons at some future time? Our instinctive response is a clear-cut negative. No person may plead that an activity designed to advance future societal benefits is justification for ignoring an immediate responsibility. Immediate needs create immediate obligations. Anticipated needs do not generate immediate, compelling obligations. The "here and now" test is a general rule of thumb which may be applied to most situations requiring an ordering of priorities.

Physicians possess skills which are not shared by other members of society. In opening a medical office or in accepting hospital appointments, they agree to make their skills available to those whom they serve. Hence, society has a unique claim upon their services, and they, in turn, bear a unique responsibility to society. The physician may not, for example, engage in strike action which compromises the health of his patients. He may not fail to attend his patient even if his motive is to effect improvement in health-care facilities or services rather than his own pecuniary self-interest. It is not legitimate for a doctor to shirk an imperative moral responsibility to patients requiring medical attention "here and now" on the plea that present nonfeasance will ultimately redound to better care for more patients at some future time. An immediate moral claim cannot be set aside in anticipation of future claims which do not as yet exist.

The physician may quite properly refuse to perform "out of title" tasks, provided such omission does not jeopardize the patient. Similarly, elective procedures which may be deferred without harm or risk do not pose an immediate obligation and may be postponed for good and sufficient reason. But, under no circumstances, may the real and immediate needs of a patient be ignored.

The obligation of society at large is, however, much broader. This enhanced obligation is reflected in a statement of the Gemara, *Baba Batra* 7b, which is cited as definitive Jewish law in *Choshen Mishpat* 163:1. Jewish law provides that the inhabitants of a city can compel one another to contribute the funds necessary for the erection of a wall around the city and for a door in the wall, as well as for bolts to secure the doors. The wall is constructed as a means of fortifying the city against armed attack. When the wall is constructed in order to preserve the lives of the inhabitants, all the townspeople may be compelled to contribute equally, since all derive equal benefit from the fortifications.

Were this an ordinary case involving immediate danger to human life, each person would be required to do all in his power to erect fortifications. At best, he would have a course of action against his fellow-townspeople for reimbursement of funds expended on their behalf—but each person capable of doing so would be required to act on his own initiative and to act without delay.

Such an obligation does not exist because, in the case in question, there is no imminent danger. Fortifications are erected, not to protect against present danger, but in anticipation of future contingencies. Precaution against future dangers is not an individual obligation but a societal obligation.

Society as a whole must see to it that there are lifeguards, physicians, and firemen trained to perform their functions and must provide facilities and incentives for the training of physicians. Any member of a society may demand that a wall be built or that locks and bolts be provided. The individual who expresses a legitimate concern with regard to possible danger which may be alleviated and a legitimate way of doing so must be heard and his demands fulfilled.

Similarly, the community has an obligation to assure that

medical services are available to rich and poor alike. While no practitioner may withhold his services because of a patient's inability to pay the required fee,[3] the individual physician is not, strictly speaking, obligated to provide such services on a general basis. The *Bet Din,* as the executive and administrative arm of society, is charged with taking any necessary measures for providing such care. The *Bet Din* may use its coercive power in ordering physicians to treat indigent patients but must see to it that the onus is shared by all available and competent physicians in an equitable manner.

Despite the awesome responsibility placed upon the physician, or perhaps *because* of it, rabbinic writings convey a certain negativism with regard to the medical profession. "The best of physicians is destined to Hell," declares the Mishnah, *Kiddushin* 82a. This statement is simply a reflection of the fact that the Talmud recognizes that individual physicians are quite prone to be remiss or negligent, on occasion, in performing their duties. Such lapses, according to Jewish teaching, occasion the severest punishment.

The physician bears responsibility not only for the physical well-being of the patient, but for his spiritual well-being as well. Old-time Jerusalemites tell an interesting anecdote about the late Dr. Wallach, of blessed memory, the founder and first medical director of Sha'arei Zedek Hospital. It was his invariable practice to visit each newly-admitted patient shortly after admission and to inquire after his or her mother's Hebrew name. Sha'arei Zedek Hospital maintains a synagogue on its premises and has instituted the laudable practice of reciting Psalms on behalf of its patients; thereafter a prayer for the recovery of each of the patients is recited. Traditionally, the prayer for the sick includes the patient's Hebrew name as well as that of the patient's mother. Hence, Dr. Wallach solicited this information and transmitted it to the synagogue sexton.

Yet Sha'arei Zedek Hospital is an efficient institution. As in all medical institutions, patients, upon admission, are required to give many details of pertinent personal information. This is followed by the recording of a medical history. Surely, another line could have been added to the admission form requesting the additional item of information and a copy routinely transmitted to the sexton! Dr. Wallach obviously wished to convey a message to the patient: This information is solicited by the medical director himself because he is fully cognizant that all healing comes from God and wishes the patient to be aware of this as well.

Rashi, in his commentary on the earlier cited Mishnah, catalogues the sins of both commission and omission common to physicians. Among them are "He gives him the diet of healthy persons to eat and does not humble his heart before God." The latter phrase is conventionally understood as referring to the excessive pride which is, at times, evidenced by physicians who erroneously come to believe that life and death are in their hands rather than in the hands of God. A more gramatically consistent interpretation, which takes cognizance of the concern manifest in Dr. Wallach's conduct, would render the translation "and does not cause him [i.e., the patient] to humble his heart before God." In failing to impress this awareness upon the patient, the physician is remiss in fulfilling the divine trust with which he is charged. In sensitizing the patient to the spiritual component inherent in the healing process the physician bears testimony to the divine purpose underlying all natural phenomena.

NOTES

1. See, for example R. Moshe Feinstein, *No'am,* VIII (5728), 9 as well as the responsum of Rabbi Feinstein which appears in the Tishri–Cheshvan 5735 issue of *Mitteilungen,* published by K'hal Adath Jeshurun of Washington Heights, New York City. *Sefer Chasidim* (*Mekitzei Nirdamim* edition, Berlin, 5651–53), no. 1469, declares that one who refrains from studying medicine for fear that he will later be inconvenienced by being called upon to treat a poor patient, or because he is fearful of committing an error, will be held culpable if a sick person dies as a result of the lack of a qualified physician. This statement should presumably be understood as expressing moral censure of unworthy motivation rather than as reflective of an absolute obligation to undertake the study of medicine.

2. See R. Eliezer Waldenberg, *Ramat Rachel,* no. 24, sec. 6; cf. *Aurkh ha-Shulchan, Yoreh De'ah* 261:6.

3. R. Eliezer Fleckles, *Teshuvah me-Ahavah,* III, *Yoreh De'ah,* no. 336; R. Shalom Schachneh, *Mishmeret Shalom,* II, 99; and R. David Katz, *Bet David,* II, *Yoreh De'ah,* no. 306.

3

Preservation of Life and Health

It is instructive to examine the physician's legal responsibilities and his moral duties as enunciated within Anglo-American secular law and within the Catholic tradition before proceeding to an analysis of Jewish moral teaching with regard to these issues.

Under the Anglo-Saxon system of law, a physician has no greater obligation to treat or advise a person in need of medical attention than has any other individual. The physician-patient relationship is viewed in common law as a contractual relationship based upon consensual agreement. While it is true that such contracts need not be expressly verbalized and exist even when the physician's services are rendered gratuitously, no obligation exists with regard to the provision of medical care unless the patient wishes medical assistance and the physician offers such treatment.

It is only after a patient is accepted for treatment that certain obligations devolve upon the physician. By submitting to examination and treatment, the patient impliedly grants permission for medical treatment and impliedly agrees to pay such professional fees as are customary and usual. By treating the patient the physician impliedly promises to continue such treatment until his professional services are no longer needed or desired by the patient. Thus, the physician-patient relationship is based upon a contract implied-in-fact.

In terms of civil law, a physician, despite his skill and licensure, is under no obligation to practice medicine, nor is he under a legal duty to render aid to another in distress. It has been conclusively established that a physician is not legally obligated to accept a patient for treatment.

Moreover, except in emergency situations, the physician is under legal constraint not to minister to the needs of the sick unless there is a clear indication on the part of the patient that treatment is desired by him. Under common law freedom from intentional unauthorized touching of the body is one of the basic freedoms enjoyed by every person. While unavoidable trespasses, such as unintentional touching in a crowded bus or elevator or the intentional grasping of a friend's arm in order to attract his attention, are accepted as part of casual social intercourse and do not constitute a personal indignity, medical procedures such as a hypodermic injection, a proctological examination or the lancing of an abscess constitute an invasion of the integrity of the person and, when unauthorized, any such action becomes an act of assault and battery. A patient who voluntarily consults a physician and voluntarily submits to treatment, relying entirely upon the physician's skill and care gives general consent by implication to at least such operation or treatment as may reasonably be necessary. The patient may at any time withdraw or limit such permission.

It has been established that prior consent of the patient is not required in life-threatening situations. In emergencies, when the patient requires immediate care to preserve life and health, the physician is reasonably privileged to treat the patient.[1] Such action is usually justified on the basis of a hypothetical assumption that were the patient competent and were it possible to seek consent without jeopardizing the patient such consent would be willingly forthcoming.

The law with regard to a physician's right to proceed *against* the expressed wishes of a fully competent patient in life-threatening situations is somewhat unsettled. Patients afflicted with terminal illnesses may, at times, express a desire for palliative treatment but indicate that they have no desire for life-prolonging therapy. In practice, physicians are often reluctant to be guided by a patient's desire because of fear not only of potential civil liability but also, under such circumstances, because of possible criminal charges. Even though the physician acts in a purely passive manner, the omission of treatment under certain circumstances constitutes manslaughter.[2]

Assuming that there exists no criminal culpability for omission of treatment on the part of the physician who has been relieved of his obligation by the patient, does the physician have the right to proceed in instituting measures designed to save the life of the patient against the wishes of the latter?

Quite a number of such cases have come before the courts via the petition of a physician or of hospital officials seeking a court order to proceed with such treatment. The vast majority of such cases involve patients who have refused medical treatment, usually in the form of blood transfusions, on religious grounds. When presented with situations in which the patient is a mentally competent adult and the resultant death will not turn the patient's children into wards of the state, the courts, for the most part, have refused to intervene.[3] The courts, in refusing to intervene, have ruled that, in the absence of a clear and present danger to society, the right to religious liberty must prevail. It is, however, firmly established that the courts are empowered to order compulsory medical treatment of minor children despite the opposition of parents based upon religious considerations.[4] In one case the court indicated that the parents of a dependent child may not refuse treatment even for themselves on the basis of religious conviction.[5] Since the parent has a responsibility to the community to care for the infant, argued the court, the people have an interest in preserving the life of the parent.

Although Scripture depicts life as a gift of God, Catholic tradition does not teach that there exists an overriding and all-encompassing obligation to preserve human life. Certainly the fifth commandment forbids the taking of life and, by implication, acts which are seriously injurious to life and perhaps even risks which involve an unreasonable likelihood of such injury. However, affirmative actions obliging one to protect and preserve bodily life or to effect a cure for debilitating illnesses and procedures designed merely to prolong life are a different matter entirely. Pius XII explicitly counseled that "Life, health, all temporal activities are in fact subordinated to spiritual ones."[6] Since preservation of life is seen as a value, but not as a paramount or overriding value, Catholic moralists teach that the obligation embraces only the use of ordinary means for the preservation of life. Life is a relative good, and the duty to preserve it is a limited one. However, employment of ordinary means is an absolute moral requirement. Failure to supply ordinary means of preserving life, albeit an act of nonfeasance, is equated with euthanasia.[7] Ordinary means are defined in the papal pronouncement as those "that do not involve any grave burden for oneself or another." In addition to being "too burdensome for most men," a more strict obligation, in the Catholic view, "would render the attainment of the higher, more important good too difficult." Extraordinary means in the preservation of life and health, i.e., measures which involve excessive difficulty by reason of physical pain, repugnance, danger or expense, etc., while not mandated by Catholic teaching, are not forbidden as long as the person employing such means "does not fail in some more serious duty."

The categories of ordinary and extraordinary are relative ones and are recognized in the papal pronouncement as varying "according to circumstances of persons, places, times and culture." In the absence of definitive concrete examples it is quite difficult to determine precisely where the point of demarcation between the two is to be drawn. Earlier authors have listed criteria which, presumably, are still applicable, e.g., leaving one's home for a more healthful climate, the amputation of a limb, all very costly treatments[8] and procedures which involve great pain.[9] Any procedure entailing grave danger of death must be considered extraordinary.[10]

The notion of ordinary means is a relative concept, determined by societal or situational considerations. The concept is nevertheless a norm established by society as a whole rather than by the individual as a subjective value. Thus, one theologian speaks of extraordinary means as those which "exceed the moral strength of men in general."[11] The judgment of ordinary versus extraordinary is to be made on the basis of how the majority of individuals would react in a given situation, allowing for the objectification of situational and subjective variables.

Significantly, mere prolongation of life is not a Catholic value. Two specific cases are discussed by the seventeenth-century Spanish Cardinal Juan De Lugo.[12] A man is unjustly condemned to death by starvation, but somehow his friends manage to get some nourishment to him. Is he obligated to eat and thereby ward off death temporarily? A man is about to be burned to death, but has a sufficient quantity of water to quench the flames which are now raging. Is he obligated to quench the fire, knowing full well that it will be rekindled by the executioner? The Cardinal answers that a person is obligated to save his life if he is capable of doing so, but he is under no obligation to put off death. Thus the condemned man is obligated to eat only if he has prospects of obtaining food on a regular basis; he must put out the flames only if there is hope that the fire will not subsequently be rekindled. De Lugo applies the principle *parum pro nihilo reputatur* and declares, "The duty of preserving one's life through ordinary means does not include the duty of using means that will prolong life so briefly that they may be morally considered as nothing."

Some Catholic theologians assert that only natural means are to be classified as ordinary and that all artificial means must be deemed extraordinary.[13] Others ignore the distinction between artificial and natural in favor of the criterion of that which is commonly used.[14]

The value with which human life is regarded in the Jewish tradition is maximized far beyond the value placed upon human life in the Christian tradition or in Anglo-Saxon common law. Jewish law bestows a privileged position upon preservation of human life as a moral value. As a moral desideratum, it takes precedence over virtually all other values. Exceptions to the general rule that preservation of life takes precedence over all other considerations are transgression of the three cardinal sins for purposes of preserving life. These are: murder (hardly an exception), idolatry, and sexual offenses such as incest and adultery. All other laws are suspended for purposes of conservation of life. Even the mere possibility of preserving life mandates suspension of biblical restrictions "however remote the likelihood of saving human life may be."[15]

These provisions reflect the unique position which preservation of life occupies in the hierarchy of values posited by Judaism. Judaism regards human life as being of infinite and inestimable value. Not only is life in general of infinite value, but every moment of life is of inestimable value as well. The quality of life which is preserved is thus never a factor to be taken into consideration. Neither is the length of the patient's life expectancy a controlling factor.

These provisions reflect a second consideration as well. One talmudic explanation of why Sabbath laws are subordinate to the preservation of life is based on the maxim, "Violate a single Sabbath on his [the patient's] behalf so that he may observe many Sabbaths" (*Yoma* 85b). Implicit in this formulation is the notion that observance of divine law must be maximized. In effect, a calculus of observance is established. Thus, temporary abrogation of ritual laws is sanctioned for the sake of enhanced observance in the future.

Ritual laws and religious observances are suspended not only in face of definite threats to life but also in the presence of "possible" or "questionable" danger. Medical advice that a given condition is, or may be, dangerous must be heeded. Some specific conditions, such as internal wounds and diseases of the eye, are described by the Talmud as inherently dangerous. These conditions must be viewed as potential threats to life even if medical science does not presently view such afflictions with the same gravity as did the Sages of the Talmud. It is quite conceivable that the talmudic assessment reflects an awareness of danger not perceived by contemporary medicine. This constitutes sufficient reason for abrogation of religious law.

As stated earlier, Judaism regards every moment of life as sacred. Hence, the patient must seek treatment, and ritual laws are suspended for the sake of such treatment even if there is no medical guarantee of a cure. Similarly, the physician's duty does *not* end when he is incapable of restoring the lost health of his patient. The obligation "And you shall restore it to him" (Deuteronomy 22:2) refers, in its medical context, not simply to the restoration of health, but to the restoration of even a single moment of life. Again, Sabbath and other laws are suspended even when it is known with certainty that human medicine offers no hope of a cure or restoration to health. Ritual obligations and restrictions are suspended so long as there is the possibility that life may be prolonged even for a matter of moments.

In the *Republic* (I, 340) Plato observes that a physician, at the time that he errs in treating a patient, is not worthy of his title. When the physician's knowledge fails him, he ceases to be a practitioner of the healing arts. Our teachers went one step further: They taught that a physician who declines to make use of his skills is not a physician; they admonished that a physician who gives up his patient as hopeless is not a physician. "*And he shall surely heal*—From here it is derived that the physician is granted permission to heal" (*Baba Kamma* 85a). To this may be added a pithy comment attributed by some to the Chassidic Seer, the *Chozeh* of Lublin, by others to the Gaon of Vilna: "The Torah gives permission to heal. It does not give the physician dispensation to refrain from healing because in his opinion the patient's condition is hopeless."

This lesson is also the moral of a story told of the nineteenth-century Polish scholar popularly known as Reb Eisel Charif. The venerable Rabbi was afflicted with a severe illness and was attended by an eminent specialist. As the disease progressed beyond hope of cure, the physician informed the Rabbi's family of the gravity of the situation. He also informed them that he therefore felt justified in withdrawing from the case. The doctor's grave prognosis notwithstanding, Reb Eisel Charif recovered completely. Some time later, the physician chanced to come upon the Rabbi in the street. The doctor stopped in his tracks in astonishment and exclaimed, "Rabbi, have you come back from the other world?" The Rabbi responded, "You are indeed correct. I *have* returned from the other world. Moreover, I did you a great favor while I was there. An angel ushered me into a large chamber. At the far end of the room was a door, and lined up in front of the door were a large number of well-dressed, dignified, and intelligent-looking men. These men were proceeding through the doorway in a single file. I asked the angel who these men were and where the door led. He informed me that the door was the entrance to the netherworld and that the men passing through those portals were those of whom the Mishnah says, 'The best of physicians merits *Gehinnom*.' Much to my surprise, I noticed that you, too, were standing in the line about to proceed through the door. I immediately approached the angel and told him: 'Remove that man immediately! He is no doctor. He does not treat patients; he abandons them!' "

To depict any human condition as hopeless is to miss entirely the spiritual dimension of human existence. Even were it true that medical diagnoses and prognoses are infallible, the decision to terminate treatment is not a medical decision; it is the determination of a moral question. That the physician possesses specialized knowledge and unique skills is unquestionable. However, his professional training guarantees neither heightened moral sensitivity nor enhanced acumen. He may quite legitimately draw medical conclusions with regard to the anticipated effects of the application or withholding of various therapeutic procedures. But the decision to proceed or not to proceed is a moral, not a medical decision. From the fact that a condition is medically hopeless it does not follow that the remaining span of life is devoid of meaning. *Nistarim darkei Ha-Shem*—"the ways of God are hidden." He has decreed that we must love, cherish, and preserve life in all its phases and guises until the very onset of death. While even terminal life is undoubtedly endowed with other meaning and value as well, subservience to the divine decree and fulfillment of God's commandment is, in itself, a matter of highest meaning.

The sanctity of human life is not predicated upon hedonistic proclivity, pragmatic utility or even upon the potential for service to one's fellow-man. The telos of human existence is service of God and the performance of His commandments. It is in this explanation of human existence that Me'iri (*Yoma* 85a) finds the rationale underlying the obligation to preserve the life of even the hopelessly ill. Me'iri observes that although the moribund patient may be incapable of any physical exertion, he may be privileged to experience contrition and utilize the precious final moments of life for the achievement of true repentance.

No scientist has ever determined the absolute (as distinct from the recordable) threshold of psychic activity. No clinical experiment has ever been conducted to determine at what level of consciousness a patient becomes incapable of remorse and repentance. But, even if possible, such an undertaking would be irrelevant. Me'iri's rationale adds a measure of understanding but does not establish the parameters of the halakhic obligation. Halakhic ramifications frequently remain operative even in situations in which the reasoning upon which they are grounded is not strictly applicable. Halakhah acquires a sanctity, *sui generis,* of its own. Human life, regardless of its quality and, indeed, of its potential for even the most minimal fulfillment of *mitzvot,* is endowed with sanctity.[16]

NOTES

1. *Luka v. Lowrie,* 171 Mich. 632; 108 N.W. 94; 7LRA (NS) 290 (1912); *Mohr v. Williams,* 95 Minn. 261, 104 N.W. 12, 15 (1905); *King v. Commonwealth,* 149 S.W. 2d 1047 (1941).

2. *People v. Beardsley,* 105 Mich. 206, 113 N.W. 1128 (1907).

3. See *Jacobson v. Mass.,* 197 U.S. 11 (1904); *People v. Pierson,* 176 N.Y. 201, 68 N.E. 243 (1903); *In re Brook's Estate,* 32 Ill. 2d 361, 205 N.E. 2d 435 (1965).

4. *People ex rel. Wallace v. Labrenz,* 411 Ill. 618, 104 N.E. 2d 769, cert. denied, 344 U.S. 824, 73 S. Ct. 24, 97 L. Ed. 642 (1952); *Morrison v. State,* Mo. App. 252 S.W. 2d 97 (1952); *Mitchell v. Davis,* Tex. Civ. App., 205 S.W. 2d 812 (1947).

5. *Application of the President and Directors of Georgetown College, Inc.,* 331 F. 2d 1000, 1008 (Washington, D.C., 1964).

6. "The Prolongation of Life," *The Pope Speaks,* IV, 395.

7. *Ethical and Religious Directives for Catholic Hospitals* (St. Louis, 1949), p. 5.

8. Gerald Kelly, S. J., "The Duty of Using Artificial Means of Preserving Life," *Theological Studies,* 11 (1950), 205.

9. Thomas J. O'Donnell, S.J., *Morals in Medicine* (Westminister, 1957), pp. 57–61. Indeed O'Donnell argues that it is the pain associated with amputation rather than the amputation *per se* which renders the procedure extraordinary. Cf. however, H. Noldin, S.J., *Summa Theologicae Moralis* (14th ed., 1922), Vol. II, n. 326, who states, ". . . the obligation [of undergoing amputation] is not to be imposed both because many have a great horror of it and . . . because it is a grave inconvenience to live with a mutilated body." O'Donnell asserts that in light of present-day surgical techniques and the perfection of artificial limbs, these considerations do not ordinarily apply.

10. See Edwin F. Healy, S.J., *Medical Ethics* (Chicago, 1956), pp. 72–74. Healy recognizes that it is difficult to express mathematically the degree of estimated danger which would render a particular procedure extraordinary. He nevertheless opines that surgery involving a mortality rate of "between 15 and 20 percent or higher" must be classified as extraordinary. Any percentage between these two norms is classified by Healy as "doubtfully ordinary" and therefore not obligatory.

11. Edwin F. Healy, S.J., *Moral Guidance* (Chicago, 1949), p. 162.

12. *De Justitia et Jure,* Disp. 10, no. 30.

13. Healy, *Medical Ethics,* p. 76.

14. Ibid., pp. 70–71.

15. *Shulchan Arukh, Orach Chaim* 329:3.

16. See *Bi'ur Halakhah, Orach Chaim* 329:4.

4

Truth-Telling

The obligation to tell the truth and to refrain from falsehood is one of the cornerstones of every ethical system. The Bible commands, "Distance yourself from a matter of falsehood" (Exodus 23:7). Yet, despite the great value placed upon truth-telling, no one would seriously advocate giving a truthful answer to *every* question. Surely, a would-be murderer seeking to discover the whereabouts of his potential victim should not be given truthful information. Every system of ethics posits not only a set of moral values, but also a means of reconciling conflicts which must inevitably arise when ethical principles come into conflict with one another. In any hierarchical ranking of values, preservation of human life is certainly far more significant than truth-telling. A lie is most assuredly warranted if that is the price which must be paid for preservation of a human life. The Talmud teaches that a "white lie" is justified for purposes of promoting tranquil relationships, for obviation of pain, embarrassment or even comparatively mild psychic distress.[1] Promotion of these goals is deemed to be of greater significance than unequivocal pursuit of truth.

In the treatment of terminal patients, the question of whether or not to divulge the nature of the disease and its prognosis is a vexing one. The patient has a certain right to information concerning himself. Indeed, the physician has, in a sense, entered into a contract with the patient to make this knowledge available to him. Often there is a genuine need for the patient to have such information available to him so that he may put his affairs in order, make provisions for his family or prepare himself spiritually for death.

On the other hand, health-care professionals have an obligation to preserve both the physical and emotional well-being of the patient. The paramount obligation of the physician is *primum non nocere,* to do no harm to the patient. The physician must be certain the information conveyed will not have a debilitating effect on his patient. It is for this reason that the third edition of the Code of Ethics of the American Medical Association, adopted in 1975, states that the physician has a sacred duty to avoid all things that have a tendency to discourage the patient and to depress his spirits. In order to prevent this from occurring, some forms of deception are justifiable.

Jewish law is particularly sensitive to the debilitating effects which mental stress may have upon an enfeebled or moribund patient. Since Judaism views every moment of life as sacred, care must be taken not to foreshorten life even by a short period of time. Thus, for example, the Gemara, *Mo'ed Katan* 26b, states that a patient should not be told of the death of a relative lest it hasten the patient's own demise.

The question of whether or not it is proper to inform a patient of his imminent demise is discussed forthrightly by the Midrash, *Kohelet Rabbah* 5:4. Isaiah was sent to inform Hezekiah that the latter's sickness was fatal (Isaiah 38:1). Hezekiah is depicted by the Midrash as reproving the prophet: "Customarily, when one visits the sick he says, 'May Heaven have mercy on you.' A physician who visits [the sick] tells him, 'This you may eat and that you may not eat. This you may drink and that you may not drink.' Even if [the physician] sees that [the patient] is about to die he does not say to him 'Leave a testament to your household' lest [the patient's] mind faint." Concern lest the patient fall prey to depression or despair and thereby death be hastened is cited by the Midrash as establishing the normative principle governing such situations.[1a] Not only must the physician refrain from transmitting information which may perchance have this effect, but he must also continue to dispense advice which has the sole effect of reassuring the patient. He must be solicitous and feign medical aid even though there is no medical purpose in his ministrations. The patient must be advised what to eat and drink—and which medicines to take—not because of the therapeutic effect of such measures, but because the significance of removal of dietary restrictions or total withdrawal of medication is not lost upon the discerning patient. The "placebo effect" of the physician's continued ministrations not only prevents despondency but has a positive psychological value which is beneficial to the patient.

The incident reported in II Kings 8:7–10 has been understood by some commentaries as illustrating precisely this concern. Ben-Hadad, the king of Aram, became sick and sent a messenger to inquire of the Prophet Elisha whether or not he would recover. Elisha informed the messenger that, in fact, Ben-Hadad would die but instructed him to tell the king, "You shall surely recover." Gersonides, commenting upon this passage, indicates that absolute candor might hasten the death of the patient. Lack of truthfulness, in such situations, is not merely permissible, or even commendable, but mandatory.[2]

The Jewish view in this matter does not parallel the well-publicized recommendations of Dr. Elisabeth Kübler-Ross.[3] Kübler-Ross based her conclusions upon information obtained through highly subjective personal interaction with some two hundred dying patients. Dr. Kübler-Ross' scientific objectivity and the validity of her conclusions have been challenged by a number of her colleagues.[4] Other researchers have reported markedly different findings.[5]

Nevertheless, whether or not Kübler-Ross' methods were scientifically sound is essentially irrelevant to our concern. Jewish teaching with regard to this issue is based on considerations which do not necessarily contradict the data upon which Dr. Kübler-Ross' findings are based. The five stages of dying, culminating in the ultimate acceptance of death without adverse physical effects, as described by Kübler-Ross, may well have been manifested by the subjects of those studies and by countless others as well. However, no universal generalization may be drawn with regard to the reactions of all patients. Not *all* patients react in the manner described by Dr. Kübler-Ross. The devastation experienced by some patients and their consequent loss of a desire to live is a repeatedly observed phenomenon. The physical effects of such psychological phenomena do not readily lend themselves to clinical analysis. The *possibility* of adverse reaction is sufficient reason for eschewing a policy of full disclosure. Jewish law is concerned with the foreshortening of even a single human life. Accordingly, in this, as in other areas of Halakhah, the possibility of hastening death in at least some patients must be the determining consideration.

Despite the growing tendency of health-care professionals to advocate that the terminally ill be made fully aware of the gravity of their condition, medical science is well aware of the adverse effects which may result from a policy of full disclosure. The halakhic consideration that *tiruf ha-da'at,* i.e., acute mental anguish, may cause or hasten death has been empirically confirmed. Medical literature contains numerous reports of deaths having no pathological cause but attributable either to fear or to despair. Dr. J. M. T. Finney, who for many years served as Professor of Surgery at the Johns Hopkins Medical School, publicly testified that his many years of experience had taught him to be selective in accepting patients. This eminent surgeon, who desired to further enhance his reputation by maintaining a low mortality rate, refused to perform major surgery upon any patient who expressed fear with regard to the success of the procedure. Dr. Finney's clinical experience led him to conclude that fear contributes to a high mortality rate.[6]

Pioneering work in collecting anthropological records of "voodoo deaths" and in presenting a medical explanation for this phenomenon was done by Dr. Walter B. Cannon. Numerous instances of death resulting from "black magic" have been reported by scientists working independently of one another among the natives of South America, Africa, Australia, New Zealand, and Haiti. Typically, the victim is overcome by misery, refuses food and drink, and literally "pines away." Many such victims were examined by competent physicians but no physical cause for their illness could be found. Post-mortem examinations produced no explanations of these deaths.

Dr. Cannon hypothesizes that in such cases demise occurs as a result of persistent excessive activity of the sympathico-adrenal system. Blood vessels constrict as a result of continuous injection of adrenaline. Resultant fall of blood pressure causes blood volume to be reduced until it becomes insufficient for maintenance of adequate circulation. Thereupon deterioration occurs in the heart and nerve centers. As a result of the damage to the organs necessary for adequate circulation they become less and less able to maintain effective blood circulation. The result is death.[7]

A series of experiments performed with rats demonstrates that hopelessness is a cause of death in animals. Wild rats were confined in a metal cage. They were then forced into a black, opaque bag in which they could not move. Later the rats were firmly grasped in order to prevent movement, removed from the bag and their whiskers and facial hair clipped in order to cause loss of stimulation. Finally, the rats were dropped into a glass jar filled with water in which the rats might swim until they were overcome by exhaustion but from which there was no escape. The procedure was designed to eliminate all hope of escape and to cause the rats to feel threatened.

A significant number of the rats died while being held in the hand; others died immediately upon being placed in the water. None of the rats survived in the water longer than fifteen minutes. Death of the rats was attributed to emotional reactions to restraint or immersion in water. However, in a control group, when hopelessness was eliminated, the rats did not die. This was achieved by repeatedly holding the rats briefly and then freeing them, and by immersing the rats in water for only a few moments on several occasions and immediately removing them from the water. The rats quickly learned that the situation was not hopeless. They became aggressive, tried to escape, and swam for much longer periods of time. Many rats swam for as long as forty to sixty hours. Clinical tests indicated a slowing of heartbeat, slowing of respiration, and lowering of body temperature among the rats which died. Autopsies revealed enlarged hearts distended with blood. Researchers who conducted this experiment attributed this type of death to overstimulation of the parasympathetic system.[8]

During World War II a considerable number of unaccountable deaths were reported among soldiers in the armed forces. Those deaths occurred among men who were apparently in good health. At autopsy no pathology could be observed. Deaths are also regularly reported among individuals who imbibe small, definitely sublethal doses of poison and among persons who inflict minor, nonlethal wounds upon themselves. In these cases the sole cause of death is simply the victims' belief in their impending doom.[9]

The fear of hastening death must, however, be carefully balanced against the patient's need to settle his affairs and to repent before death. Accordingly, the *Shulchan Arukh*[10] rules that a patient should be instructed to turn his attention to his affairs, to make appropriate arrangements in the event that "he has lent or deposited money with others or others have lent or deposited money with him," but adds that the patient must explicitly be told that such instructions should not be construed as an indication that death is imminent. Similarly, a patient should be told to repent and to confess his sins, but must be counseled that "many have confessed and have not died, while many who have not confessed have died."[11]

Rabbi Abraham Danzig, author of the authoritative compendium, *Chokhmat Adam,* reports with approbation a custom which was followed in Berlin and a number of other Jewish communities.[12] The officers of the *Chevrah Kaddisha* were wont to pay a visit to all persons on the third day of their illness. Upon arrival, they informed the patient that it was their custom to pay such a visit to all who fell sick regardless of the severity of the illness and thereby endeavored to relieve any anxiety their visit might occasion. They then spoke to the patient regarding the matters outlined in the *Shulchan Arukh.* Since this was an established custom, neither the visit nor the conversation was viewed with apprehension. The practice followed by the *Chevrah Kaddisha* of the Berlin community may well be used as a model by present-day physicians. The physician, when treating a patient suffering from what may possibly be a serious malady, may wish to impart the same temporal and spiritual advice which was offered by the *Chevrah Kaddisha.* He should make it clear to the patient that he offers identical advice to all of his patients, and that he does so routinely, not only when he "fears the worst." In this way, the patient will neither be lulled into a false sense of security nor will he perceive a cause for undue alarm.

The way in which information is imparted, the language, tone of voice, and facial expression are as significant as the message itself. The physician must never convey the feeling that there is no hope. Indeed, such a message constitutes an untruth, for remission and even recovery have occurred even in the face of the gravest prognosis. By the same token, the physician, when dealing with an intelligent and mentally stable patient, should not give the impression that *any* illness is devoid of danger. That, too, is simply not the case.

There is no need to convey a precise diagnosis to the patient, when such information can reasonably be withheld, if the patient will identify the diagnosed condition with a terminal malady. When the patient is aware of the gravity of his condition, the physician should always be encouraging and positive in his approach. He should stress the positive aspects of available modes of therapy and, by word and action, encourage the patient not to abandon hope. This is not to say that the doctor should guarantee either recovery or longevity. He should, rather, endeavor to bolster the spirits of his patients without denying the possibility of serious developments. Above all, the physician's tone and demeanor should at all times be hopeful and supportive.

NOTES

1. See *Pesikta Zutrati, Parshat Va-Yechi; Baba Metzia* 23b; and *Ketubot* 17a.

1a. Cf. *Sefer Chasidim,* no. 154 and R. Abraham Price, *Mishnat Avraham, ad loc.*

2. See Rabbi Betzalel Stern, *Teshuvot be-Tzel ha-Chokhmah,* II, no. 55; and *She'arim ha-Metzuyanim be-Halakhah* 191:2.

3. *On Death and Dying* (New York, 1969) and *Questions and Answers on Death and Dying* (New York, 1974).

4. Richard Schultz and David Aderman, "Clinical Research and the Stages of Dying," *Omega,* V (1974), 137–143; and Roy Branson, "Is Acceptance a Denial of Death? Another Look at Kübler-Ross," *Christian Century,* May 7, 1975, pp. 464–468. See also *Time,* Nov. 12, 1979, p. 81.

5. See J. M. Hinton, "The Physical and Mental Distress of Dying," *Quarterly Journal of Medicine,* XXXII (1963), 1–21; and K. A. Achte and M. L. Vaukkonen, "Cancer and the Psyche," *Omega,* II (1971), 46–56.

6. Walter B. Cannon, " 'Voodoo' Death," *American Anthropologist,* vol. XLIV (1942), no. 2; reprinted in *Psychosomatic Medicine,* vol. XIX (1957), no. 3, p. 189.

7. Ibid., pp. 182–190.

8. Curt P. Richter, "On the Phenomenon of Sudden Death in Animals and Man," *Psychosomatic Medicine,* vol. XIX (1957), no. 3, pp. 191–198.

9. Ibid., p. 197.

10. *Yoreh De'ah* 335:7.

11. Ibid., 338:1.

12. *Chokhmat Adam* 151:10.

5

Professional Secrecy

Judaism places stringent restrictions upon disclosure of confidential information, regardless of whether the information is received in the course of a professional relationship, as a confidential non-professional communication, as the result of an inadvertent or accidental disclosure, or through a third party.

The prohibition against divulging personal information concerning another person is derived from the biblical verse "You shall not go as a bearer of tales among your people (Leviticus 19:16). Such activity is forbidden even when it is not accompanied by malicious intent and even if the information is not derogatory in nature. As formulated by Maimonides, "Who is a tale-bearer? One who carries reports and goes from one person to another and says, 'So-and-so said this' or 'Such and such have I heard about so-and so.' Even if he tells the truth, [the tale-bearer] destroys the world."[1]

The prohibition against disclosure of information of a personal nature would appear to yield canons of professional confidentiality even more restrictive than those reflected in presently accepted codes of professional conduct. In some ways this is indeed true. However, Jewish law acknowledges that in certain circumstances even professional confidences must be revealed. Disclosure of medical information, in particular, is discussed in detail in a work entitled *Chafetz Chaim,* a classic text which deals with Jewish law as applied to slander, defamation of character, tale-bearing, and the like.

The particular situation discussed by the author of *Chafetz Chaim*[2] is that of a person seeking disclosure of medical information concerning a prospective marriage partner. *Chafetz Chaim* rules that, in principle, such information may be divulged. Disclosure is, however, restricted in the following four ways: (1) The presence of a disease or physical defect may be disclosed. However, a vague, general weakness or deficiency which does not directly compromise health may not be disclosed. (2) The nature or extent of a disease or injury must not be exaggerated in any way. (3) The sole motivation prompting disclosure must be the benefit of the person to whom the information is supplied. No disclosure may be made when prompted, even in part, by personal animosity. (4) Disclosure is permissible only when there exist reasonable grounds for assuming that the information divulged will be the determining factor in terms of the contemplated marriage. Such information may not be divulged unless there is reason to assume that the ultimate decision will be affected thereby.

These provisions of Jewish law apply not only to disclosure of information with regard to a prospective marriage partner but, *mutatis mutandis,* are applicable with regard to disclosure of information to a prospective employer as well. It is quite evident that these provisions of Halakhah reflect a balance between considerations of privacy and considerations of potential harm or damage which may occur to another party. No person has the right to divulge information of a personal nature concerning a fellow human being simply in order to satisfy the curiosity of a third party. By the same token, such information cannot legitimately be disclosed simply in order to make a dossier complete. The crucial consideration is the "need to know" in the sense of avoiding potential harm, loss or damage. It follows, therefore, that, for example, information which has no bearing upon job performance may not be revealed. Since the information in question is not necessary to prevent harm or financial loss, the privacy of such information may not be violated.

Respect for privacy and the inviolability of the professional relationship certainly do not take precedence over protection of the lives and safety of others. The overriding obligation to protect the lives of others is of sufficient weight to oblige the physician to take whatever measures may be necessary to eliminate the danger. Thus, for example, a physician must inform the motor vehicle bureau that his patient is an epileptic and should be denied a driver's license.[3] The obligation to violate the confidential nature of the physician-patient relationship in such extreme situations is encompassed within the provisions of the "law of pursuit." A person engaged in an activity which will lead to the death of another must be prevented from causing such death, even though the potentially tragic consequences are entirely unintentional. An automobile driver suffering from a condition such as epilepsy endangers the lives of innocent persons. Any person aware of this fact, regardless of how he comes into possession of such information, is under obligation to take any measures deemed to be reasonable and necessary in order to preserve the lives of potential victims.

Accordingly, the recipient of a privileged communication is obliged to disclose information imparted to him in order to preserve the lives and property of others. If, however, no danger exists, or if the danger can be averted by other means, he may not violate the confidence. The desire to see an evildoer brought to justice and punished for his crime is not, in itself, sufficient reason to justify breach of confidence. When it is necessary to disclose information, disclosure must be limited to those facts and details which require disclosure in order to obviate danger.

Jewish law also provides that a *Bet Din* may compel testimony which entails revelation of a personal or professional confidence. The obligation born of the commandment ". . . he who is a witness . . . if he does not inform, he shall bear his iniquity" (Leviticus 5:1) supersedes the obligation to respect the privacy of others. In such instances Jewish law would require that testimony of this nature be heard *in camera* in order that matters of a personal nature not be overheard by persons who have no "need to know."

NOTES

1. *Hilkhot De'ot* 7:2.
2. *Hilkhot Issurei Rekhilut, Klal* 9.
3. See R. Ovadiah Yosef, *Yechaveh Da'at,* IV, no. 60.

6

Kohanim *as Medical and Dental Students*

The descendants of Aaron are forbidden to come into contact with, or to be under the same roof as, a dead body, except in the case of the death of a close relative (Leviticus 21:1). Contact with a corpse gives rise to a state of ritual impurity which may be purged only by means of a process of purification spanning a period of seven days. Water mixed with the ashes of the red heifer is sprinkled upon the person undergoing the rite of purification on the third and seventh day. A person in a state of ritual impurity may not partake of sacrificial offerings and may not enter the Temple precincts (Numbers 19:1–13).

Maimonides explains that *kohanim* are forbidden to come into contact with a corpse because they are charged with performing the sacrificial rites in the Temple.[1] Priests constantly had occasion to enter the Temple and hence were forbidden to become ritually impure in a manner which would debar them from entry into the Temple for an entire week. Although the Temple is destroyed, and Israel is in exile, this prohibition remains fully in effect. Adherence to the laws of priestly purity is but one of the manifold expressions of the faith of the Jewish people in the redemption of Israel. Since the advent of the Messiah and the rebuilding of the Temple are awaited with eager anticipation, *kohanim* are charged to maintain themselves in a constant state of preparedness so that, at the awaited moment, they will be able immediately to resume their priestly duties.

Thus, effectively, a *kohen* is forbidden to participate in the anatomy dissections which are an integral part of medical and dental school curricula. Halakhic problems are also posed for *kohanim* in the practice of medicine since they may be called upon to be in hospital buildings for purposes not related to *pikuach nefesh.* Not only is a *kohen* forbidden to come into physical contact with a dead body but he is also forbidden to be in the same "tent," or room, as a corpse. In many circumstances the *kohen* is not permitted entry into the entire building. He is also forbidden to enter a hospital or other building at such time as a *goses,* i.e., a moribund patient in imminent danger of death, is on the premises.

The restrictions against touching a dead body apply to the corpse of a gentile as well as to that of a Jew. Although some authorities differ, both *Shulchan Arukh* and Rema, *Yoreh De'ah* 372:2, rule that proper comportment requires a *kohen* to exercise vigilance in avoiding contact with the grave of a non-Jew. Thus, not only is the *kohen* forbidden to touch the corpse of a non-Jew but he is also forbidden to be present in the same "tent" as the body of a non-Jew. The halakhic principle recorded in this ruling is that the body of a non-Jew causes ritual impurity in exactly the same manner as does that of a Jew; viz., both by means of tactile contact and by presence under a single roof. Therefore, according to this ruling, it is not only forbidden for a *kohen* himself to perform an anatomy dissection, but it is also improper for him to be present in the laboratory together with a non-Jewish cadaver. Thus, even assuming that the cadaver to be dissected is indeed that of a non-Jew, and even if the *kohen* were able to satisfy the laboratory requirement by simply observing others perform the anatomy dissection, it would be improper for him to be in the same room as a non-Jewish cadaver.[2]

It is indeed true that one authority, Rabad, *Hilkhot Nezirut* 5:15, does express the opinion that the prohibition against *tumat kohanim* is mitigated in our day. His position is predicated upon the consideration that in the absence of the ashes of the red heifer, which are necessary for the purification ritual, a person who has become ritually impure through contact with a corpse remains permanently in a state of impurity. Accordingly, argues Rabad, additional contact with a corpse does not add to the state of impurity. One latter-day authority, R. Akiva

Eger, *Teshuvot R. Akiva Eger, Mahadura Tinyana,* no. 18, maintains that, according to Rabad, there exists no prohibition whatsoever against a *kohen* coming into contact with a corpse if he has indeed previously become ritually impure.[3]

However, in light of Rabad's own statement in his responsa collection, *Temim De'im,* no. 236, to the effect that a biblical prohibition against *tumat kohanim* does exist even in our day, Rabad's gloss on the *Mishneh Torah* must be understood as referring only to the punishment of *malkot,* or lashes, administered for infraction of a biblical prohibition. Indeed, Rabad, *Hilkhot Nezirut* 5:15, speaks only of the absence of a *chiyuv tumah,* i.e., punitive culpability. Thus Rabad's position is that "additional" defilement *is* biblically prohibited, although not punishable by the *Bet Din.*[4] Rabad's position is understood in precisely this manner by R. Ezekiel Landau, *Dagul me-Revavah, Yoreh De'ah* 372:2, and by *Teshuvot Chatam Sofer, Yoreh De'ah,* no. 338.[5] In any event, Rabad's position is an isolated opinion and is contradicted by the vast majority of halakhic decisors who maintain that each additional act of defilement constitutes a separate transgression. Their position is certainly in accordance with the obvious import of the discussion of this matter recorded in *Nazir* 42b.

Recently, one writer has argued that, despite this prohibition, *kohanim* may be permitted to study medicine because such study leads to *pikuach nefesh,* the saving of lives of patients who will be treated in the course of the physician's professional career.[6] This argument is sharply and peremptorily dismissed by R. Moshe Feinstein in a responsum which appeared in the Tishri–Cheshvan 5735 issue of *Mitteilungen,* the congregational bulletin of K'hal Adath Jeshurun of Washington Heights, New York City. It is a well-established principle of Jewish law that halakhic restrictions are suspended only in face of an already existing danger to life. Halakhic prohibitions may not be disregarded simply because of the possibility that some emergency may perhaps arise. Such vague contingencies do not constitute *pikuach nefesh.* This principle will be examined in greater detail in chapter 27. Thus there is no obligation on the part of any individual to undertake the study of medicine in order that he may be qualified to treat someone who may become ill at some future time. It then follows unquestionably that no halakhic strictures may be violated in the course of pursuing a medical education.[7] It is therefore forbidden for a *kohen* to violate the prohibition against *tumat met* just as it is forbidden to engage in forbidden activities on *Shabbat* in order to receive a medical education.

The serious nature of the infraction of the strictures against *tumat kohanim* is reflected in the halakhic provision which bars a *kohen* who ignores this prohibition from being accorded the honors attendant upon his status. Thus *Shulchan Arukh, Orach Chaim* 128:41, provides that a *kohen* who habitually comes in contact with the dead may not be permitted to recite the priestly blessing nor is he to be accorded the distinction of being called first to the reading of the Torah, as is the privilege of *kohen*.

The question of whether these honors may be accorded to a physician or medical student who comes into contact with corpses (other than in instances of possible *pikuach nefesh*) was first discussed by R. Yehudah Asad, *Teshuvot Yehudah Ya'aleh*, no. 47. This authority expresses the opinion that it is inconceivable that a *kohen* would wantonly compromise the sanctity of his priestly office. It should therefore be assumed that the *kohen* either erroneously believes that the prohibition does not include contact with the corpses of non-Jews or else is misguided in assuming that considerations of *pikuach nefesh* apply to the study of medicine. Accordingly, he concludes, "It is incumbent to speak with him gently and to show him the law [which is] explicit in *Shulchan Arukh*." In accordance with the provisions recorded in *Shulchan Arukh*, Mahari Asad rules that the *kohen* must enter into a solemn undertaking in the presence of a *Bet Din* giving assurance that he will no longer disregard this prohibition. Mahari Asad rules that in the absence of such an undertaking the *kohen* may not be accorded these dignities.

Another authority, R. Abraham Benjamin Sofer, *Teshuvot Ketav Sofer, Orach Chaim*, no. 16, notes that in the case of a *kohen* who has entered into a forbidden marriage, divorce and a simple declaration not to repeat the transgression are not sufficient. Before he may once more be accorded the honors associated with the priestly office, the *kohen* must solemnly vow—in a manner such that the vow cannot subsequently be annulled—not to repeat his misdeed. *Ketav Sofer* argues that, similarly, since a physician derives financial remuneration for services rendered in conjunction with defilement through contact with the deceased, a solemn vow may be required rather than a simple declaration.

R. David Hoffman, *Teshuvot Melamed le-Ho'il, Orach Chaim,* no. 31, states that such honors may be accorded a *kohen* who has inadvertently transgressed this prohibition. He rules, however, that should the *kohen* persist in such conduct it is forbidden to continue to accord him the honor of the first *aliyah* since bestowal of such honor "strengthens his hand" in ongoing violations of Halakhah. *Melamed le-Ho'il* concludes with the statement that only if it is known that the *gabbai,* who is responsible for assigning synagogue honors, will fail to conform to the dictates of Jewish law is it permissible to remain silent, so that the *gabbai's* transgression remains inadvertent rather than willful.

NOTES

1. *Guide of the Perplexed,* book III, chap. 47.
2. See *Avnei Nezer, Yoreh De'ah,* II, no. 467, and R. Yechiel Michal Tucatzinsky, *Gesher ha-Chaim,* I, chap. 6, sec. 3.
3. See also R. Yitzchak ben Yosef ha-Kohen, *Ohel Yitzchak,* no. 33.
4. See also *Teshuvot ha-Rashba,* I, nos. 324 and 410; *Sha'ar ha-Zekenim,* II, 125; and *Mishneh le-Melekh, Hilkhot Nezerut* 5:15. Ramban, *Makkot* 21a, also cites Rabad as asserting that no punishment is imposed but that defilement in our day is forbidden nevertheless.
5. See also *Teshuvot Chatam Sofer, Orach Chaim,* no. 23; R. Moshe Zevi Fuchs, *Teshuvot Yad Ramah,* no. 128; and R. Yehudah Leib Zirelson, *Gevul Yehudah, Yoreh De'ah,* no. 31. Other rabbinic scholars, who apparently were unaware of Rabad's statement in *Temim De'im,* understood his gloss on the *Mishneh Torah* as referring to the biblical prohibition only. According to their understanding, Rabad viewed "additional" defilement as forbidden by virtue of rabbinic edict. Among these authorities are *Teshuvot Zemach Zedek,* no. 238; *Yeshu'ot Ya'akov, Orach Chaim* 343:2; and *Shiyurei Korban,* Palestinian Talmud, *Nazir* 3:1.
6. See R. Mordecai ha-Kohen, *Sinai,* vol LIV, no. 1–2 (Tishri-Cheshvan 5724), pp. 40–46, reprinted in *Torah she-be-al Peh,* VI (5724), 74–81, and *Machanayim,* no. 123 (Kislev 5730), pp. 120–129.
7. Additional discussions of the issues involved in the question of the study and practice of medicine by *kohanim* appear in *Teshuvot*

Yehudah Ya'aleh, no. 47; *Nachal Eshkol,* introduction, pp. 11–13; *Teshuvot Shevut Ya'akov, Yoreh De'ah,* no. 85; *Teshuvot Gevul Yehudah, Yoreh De'ah* no. 31; R. Elazar Meir Preil, *Yagdil Torah,* VIII (5676), 3–8; R. Bernard Revel, *Yagdil Torah,* VIII (5676), 85–90; R. Elyakim Goldberg, *Yagdil Torah,* VIII (5676), 19–21, 135–141, and 256–259; R. Chaim Hirschenson, *Malki ba-Kodesh,* III, no. 5; R. Yekutiel Yehudah Greenwald, *Kol Bo al Aveilut,* pp. 81–84; and R. Shmuel Hibner, *Ha-Darom,* Elul 5721, pp. 17–28, reprinted in R. Shmuel Hibner, *Nemukei Shmu'el,* pp. 192–205.

7

Visiting the Sick

Bikkur cholim, or visiting the sick, is much more than a commendable social act. Jewish law endows *bikkur cholim* with the status of a *mitzvah.* In and of itself, it constitutes the fulfillment of a divine commandment.

This *mitzvah* can be traced directly to the solicitude evidenced by God Himself in visiting Abraham during his period of convalescence following circumcision. Genesis 18:1 records that God appeared before Abraham but fails to report any particular prophetic revelation. The Midrash explains that the event occurred on the third day following Abraham's circumcision and that the divine appearance was simply for purposes of visiting the sick.

Scripture commands, "And you shall walk in His ways" (Deuteronomy 28:9). Man is bidden to pattern himself, insofar as humanly possible, upon the ways of God. The doctrine of *imitatio Dei,* which is predicated upon this verse, posits an obligation to emulate God. It establishes that man's goal in this world is to serve God by making his life a model of divinely revealed values: "As He is merciful, even so be you merciful. As He is gracious, even so be you gracious." The Gemara, *Sotah* 14a, explicitly extends this concept to encompass visiting the sick: "As He clothes the naked . . . so you clothe the naked. The Holy One, blessed be He, visits the sick, as it is written, 'And God appeared to him at Elonei Mamre,' so you visit the sick."

The *mitzvah* of visiting the sick devolves upon every individual. Historically, Jewish communities established societies whose members undertook the responsibility of performing this sacred task. This was done, not to exempt others, but to assure that ample provision would always be made for the needs of the sick. To this very day, the presence of an active *Bikkur Cholim* society is a hallmark of a vibrant Jewish community. The notion that visiting the sick is a duty falling especially upon the rabbi or chaplain is foreign to Judaism. This, of course, does not mean that rabbis are exempt from the *mitzvah*. It is reported that the renowned Rabbi Akiva Eger, whose diligence in Torah study and extreme reluctance to spend precious moments in other activities are well documented, made it a constant practice personally to visit the sick. Frequently, he would spent the entire night at the bedside of a critically ill patient.[1]

The *mitzvah* of *bikkur cholim* requires something quite different from a "visit" in the sense of a social call. Nachmanides explains that the *mitzvah* consists of two parts: (1) an endeavor to determine whether the patient requires care and actual provision of such medical or nursing care as may be necessary; and (2) prayer on behalf of the patient. Direct personal contact with the patient enables the visitor to empathize with the needs of the patient and to pray with greater sincerity. Nachmanides concludes with the comment, "One who visits the sick and does not pray on his behalf has not fulfilled the *mitzvah*."[2] This halakhic ruling is recorded by Rema, *Yoreh De'ah* 335:4. To be sure, a patient's needs may be psychological rather than physical. A visitor who provides companionship and a cheering word when needed has certainly performed a service on behalf of the patient. Alleviation of physical pain may be beyond human control, but easing psychological anguish is within the power of all. Man's complex psychological and physical responses interact in a subtle manner. A patient's mental outlook has a marked effect upon recuperation. The knowledge that others care and their offer of encouragement may motivate a patient to marshal flagging resources and renew his fight for life. However, a mere social call paid to a patient who has no desire or need for such solicitude does not constitute a *mitzvah* unless designed to stimulate prayer on the patient's behalf. It should be emphasized that the visitor must be sensitive to the individual patient's condition and needs. Visits which are tiring or otherwise lead to discomfort for the patient should not be undertaken.

One is certainly obligated to provide for the religious needs of a patient not only by virtue of the general obligation which Jews have with regard to one another and because they are charged with assisting others in performing *mitzvot,* but also because lack of an opportunity to perform a *mitzvah* can often have a deleterious effect upon the mental outlook of the patient. Thus, the patient's needs with regard to blowing of the *shofar, lulav* and *etrog,* reading the *megillah,* etc., should be accommodated not only for religious reasons, but on therapeutic grounds as well.

In particular, provision should be made for the kindling of Sabbath candles and the Channukah *menorah.* The psychological significance of being able to fulfill these *mitzvot* and the trauma to the observant patient engendered by their omission is of therapeutic significance and should evoke a sympathetic response on the part of medical personnel and hospital administrators. When Sabbath candles cannot be used, e.g., in a room in which oxygen is being administered, electric substitutes should be utilized.[3]

Patients, particularly those suffering from serious illnesses, are exempt from many provisions of Jewish law. A competent rabbi should be consulted with regard to specific questions which may arise. In general, however, it must be stated that Judaism sees no value in, and indeed discourages, ceremonies and rituals which do not constitute fulfilment of a *mitzvah* in its proper form. Thus, for example, the Passover *seder* may be conducted only after nightfall. A *seder* during the late afternoon of *erev Pesach* is of no religious significance. Indeed, eating *matzah* prior to the proper time for the *seder* is actually forbidden. These provisions of Jewish law are not suspended simply to satisfy a subjective desire to participate in Passover observances.

Public prayer with a *minyan* is certainly meritorious, and if possible, hospital patients should be accorded the opportunity to pray in this manner. It must, however, be emphasized that all such services must be conducted in accordance with the provisions of Jewish law. Morning services, for example, should be held only during the hours designated by *Shulchan Arukh.* A patient who has difficulty reciting the entire prayer service should consult a rabbi for guidance. Public services on behalf of patients which are abbreviated in nature are, in general, contrary to Jewish law. Such services should not be introduced without competent rabbinic guidance. Under no circumstances may a Jew operate an elevator on *Shabbat* or *Yom Tov* in order to enable a patient to participate in communal worship. Use by a patient of an elevator which is operated by a non-Jew involves complex questions of Jewish law. Since these questions involve matters with regard to which there exist significant differences of opinion and which depend, at least in part, upon the nature of the electrical mechanism utilized, a competent rabbinic authority should be consulted. It should be stated, however, that the question can be considered only for purposes of enabling the patient to participate in *tefillah be-tzibbur*—communal prayer with a *minyan* in its proper form as defined by Jewish law.

Attention to the needs of the patient, whether they be medical, physical, psychological or spiritual, constitutes the essence of the *mitzvah* of *bikkur cholim,* of which the Sages declared, "The fruits are enjoyed in this world, while the principal remains for the World to Come" (*Pe'ah* 1:1). The meticulous concern for human needs mandated by this *mitzvah* is one of the loftiest expressions of the love for one's fellow enjoined by the Torah.

NOTES

1. Rabbi Shlomo Sofer, *Chut ha-Meshulash he-Chadash* (Tel Aviv, 5723), p. 207.
2. Nachmanides, *Torat ha-Adam,* in *Kitvei Ramban,* ed. Charles B. Chavel (Jerusalem, 5723), II, 17.
3. Since there is significant difference of opinion with regard to reciting the blessing over electric lights, the patient should consult his or her rabbi with regard to this question if it is impossible to light candles in the usual manner.

8

Circumcision

Brit milah, the covenant of circumcision, is one of the most fundamental rituals of Judaism. The *brit milah* constitutes a reaffirmation of the covenant between God and the descendants of Abraham. The act of circumcision stamps the Jew with the sign of the covenant and testifies to his unique status as the bearer of divinely imposed responsibilities. Rabbinic literature is replete with additional suggestions concerning the symbolism represented in the rite of circumcision. Of particular significance is the concept that the removal of the foreskin, which constitutes a physical obstruction, is symbolic of the removal of the spiritual barrier which may separate the heart of man from God.

Circumcision is, of course, a surgical procedure, but, for Jews, it is fundamentally a religious obligation and differs significantly in the manner of its performance from the various techniques commonly employed in surgical circumcision. Halakhah stipulates that circumcision must be performed by a pious Jew who is meticulous in his observance of the tenets of Judaism. Under no circumstances may a non-Jew perform the rite of *milah* upon a Jewish child. The essence of the commandment is the removal of the foreskin and the underlying membrane known as the *or ha-pri'ah.* As is the case with regard to the performance of other *mitzvot,* an appropriate blessing is recited. Since the severing of the foreskin constitutes the essence of the *mitzvah,* the practice of having a non-Jewish or non-observant physician perform the circumcision in the presence of a rabbi or other person who pronounces the blessing is not acceptable according to Jewish law.

Milah must be performed with a sharp cutting instrument. Tradition prescribes that a double-edged knife, rather than, for example, a scalpel, be used for this purpose. This custom is based upon the verse "Let the praise of God be in their mouth and a double-edged sword in their hand" (Psalms 149:6), which is interpreted as an allusion to the rite of circumcision. This practice serves to prevent the possible discomfort to the child that might result from inadvertent application of the blunt side of the knife to the foreskin. Use of a single-edged instrument does not, however, render the *milah* invalid.[1]

A clamp or similar device which causes the foreskin to atrophy before removal or which interferes with the free flow of blood should not be used. The use of the Gumco clamp was formally interdicted by a pronouncement issued by the Union of Orthodox Rabbis of the United States and Canada dated 12 Tevet 5711.[2] The selfsame considerations apply to the use of similar devices, including the *Magen,* when applied as designed for purposes of cutting off the blood supply to the foreskin.[3] A metal protective shield which holds the foreskin in place, but does not cause the foreskin to atrophy, may be used.

Milah is performed on the eighth day subsequent to parturition, even when the eighth day falls on the Sabbath, a Festival or *Yom Kippur.* Circumcision is one of the few *mitzvot* whose fulfillment takes precedence over Sabbath restrictions. However, only the act of circumcision supersedes such restrictions; preparatory acts, such as boiling of instruments or forbidden travel, may not be undertaken on the Sabbath or on the first two or last two days of a Festival even if as a result circumcision must be delayed. *Milah* must be performed during daylight hours. Under no circumstances should *milah* be performed at night or prior to the eighth day.

Milah should, and indeed must, be postponed beyond the eighth day whenever medically indicated. If circumcision is delayed for any serious medical consideration, seven full days must elapse subsequent to the complete recovery of the child before circumcision may be performed.

At times, Jewish law requires postponement of circumcision even though contemporary medical science recognizes no potential threat to the health of the baby. The most common example of such a situation is the presence of physiological jaundice as evidenced by yellowness of the skin. Circumcision should not be performed in such cases even though the physician may quite appropriately advise that there exists no known danger. However, when circumcision is delayed for reason of yellowness of this nature, a seven-day waiting period is not required. Circumcision should never be delayed beyond the time required by Jewish law. Nevertheless, when circumcision does not take place on the eighth day, it may not be performed on a Sabbath or Festival. Similarly, the circumcision of a child delivered by cesarean section may not be performed on a Sabbath or Festival. For a similar reason, circumcision of a child born between sunset and nightfall of Friday evening or of the eighth day preceding a Festival may not be performed on the Sabbath or on a Festival. In each of these instances the circumcision should be performed on the day immediately following the Sabbath or Festival.

At times, it may be necessary to delay circumcision in order to provide for correction of a congenital defect. In a normal male the urethra, i.e., the canal or passage through which urine is discharged, extends through the entire length of the male organ and opens at the tip of the glans. In approximately one out of every three hundred male births a congenital anomaly known as hypospadias occurs. Hypospadias is a congenital defect involving a developmental anomaly characterized by a defect in the wall of the urethra. As a result of this anomaly, the canal does not terminate in an orifice at the tip of the organ but opens instead on the under surface, either at a point close to the glans or elsewhere along the length of the organ or, at times, close to or even in the scrotum itself. This condition is frequently accompanied by either an abbreviated or a displaced foreskin, which may at times leave the underside of the glans completely exposed and often gives the child the appearance of being partially circumcised. In rare cases the opening may be on the upper surface of the organ, a condition known as epispadias. Depending upon the location of the orifice, the male may not be able to experience ejaculation in the usual manner in conjunction with sexual intercourse and hence may not be able to sire children.

Contemporary medical practice is to delay repair of this condition until the child is approximately three years of age. At that time an epithelial tube is constructed in place of the missing segment of the urethra and the congenital anomalous orifice is closed. Physicians advise against circumcision prior to the time of surgery so that the foreskin will be available for use as a skin flap for transfer in conjunction with the reconstructive plastic surgery necessary for correction of hypospadias.

Since performance of *milah* on the eighth day may preclude such corrective surgery and thereby make it impossible for the child ever to sire children, circumcision can be delayed in order to remedy the condition.[4] Surgical correction, however, is not medically necessary, or even advisable, in all cases. The need for corrective surgery is determined by the location of the orifice. Accordingly, every case of hypospadias should be evaluated by urologists specializing in the correction of this condition. Moreoever, a competent rabbinic authority should be consulted for advice with regard to performance of the *mitzvah* of *milah* in the proper manner in conjunction with reconstructive surgery.

NOTES

1. See *Derekh Pekudekha,* no. 2, *chelek ha-ma'aseh,* sec. 30.
2. See *Ha-Pardes,* vol. 25, no. 5 (Shevat 5711), p. 31.
3. See, for example, R. Moshe Sternbuch, *Dat ve-Halakhah* (Jerusalem, 5730), no. 2; and R. Moshe B. Pirutinsky, *Sefer ha-Brit* (New York, 5732), *Likkutei Halakhot* 264:76.
4. See *Avnei Nezer, Yoreh De'ah,* II, nos. 321 and 322; *Teshuvot Tirosh ve-Yitzhar,* nos. 97 and 127; *Teshuvot Atzei ha-Levanon,* no. 61; *Teshuvot Chelkat Ya'akov,* II, nos. 20 and 21, and III, nos. 36 and 37; and R. Moshe B. Pirutinsky, *Sefer ha-Brit, Likkutei Halakhot* 261:47–48, *Sefer ha-Brit, Mekor u-Biur Halakhah* 261:5, and *Sefer ha-Brit,* second edition, (New York, 5738), addenda, p. 415.

9

Population Control

The attitude of Judaism toward population control is shaped by two considerations, one negative, the other positive. The negative consideration is rooted in the biblical condemnation of onanism (Genesis 38:9–10) and is predicated upon a prohibition against destruction of the male seed. There is, however, a positive consideration as well. The scriptural injunction "Be fruitful and multiply" (Genesis 9:7) is regarded not simply as a blessing but as a directive. Indeed, Judaism views this commandment as the first of the 613 biblically ordained commandments. Thus, Jewish teaching, while allowing for exceptions in limited circumstances, is inherently biased against birth control measures.

According to rabbinic interpretation, the obligation with regard to procreation is fulfilled by the siring of two children, one male and one female, provided that each of the two in turn becomes the parent of both a boy and a girl. Nevertheless, further procreation is regarded as meritorious. "In the morning sow your seed, and in the evening withhold not your hand" (Ecclesiastes 11:6) is understood by the Talmud as an exhortation to engage in procreation not only in the "morning" of life, but also in the "evening" of life, i.e., even after statutory requirements have already been fulfilled.

These provisions of Halakhah are firmly rooted in Jewish theology. The Gemara, *Chagigah* 2b, declares, "For indeed the universe was created solely for procreation, as it is said, 'He created it not a waste. He formed it to be inhabited' " (Isaiah 45:18). The divine scheme provides for natural increase in the population of the world because the telos of creation cannot be fulfilled other than through God's creatures. Moreover, another talmudic source indicates that the coming of the Messiah and the redemption of mankind will not occur until the created world has been fully populated in accordance with the divine plan. Failure to procreate is seen not merely as a violation of divine law but as an impediment to the coming of the Messiah. The Gemara, *Niddah* 13b, teaches that the redemption will not occur until there remain no unborn souls, i.e., until all potential human life becomes actual.

Concomitantly, belief in divine providence leads to the assumption that earth's natural resources, coupled with innovative human technology, can support the world population. From this perspective, the problem to which humanity is morally bound to address itself is not the problem of overpopulation but the problem of maldistribution of resources. The oft-quoted dictum "He who gives life gives sustenance" is an affirmation of faith in the divine commitment to the human race. He who bestows the gift of life undertakes to provide the necessities of existence.

While the Talmud advises abstinence during periods of famine, this counsel is not designed primarily as a means of containing population growth but is predicated upon the unseemliness of engaging in acts of physical gratification at a time when the populace is in distress. Indeed, specific exception is made for the night of the wife's ritual immersion following the menstrual period, a time regarded by the Sages of the Talmud as most likely to lead to conception.

A number of contemporary Jewish thinkers have urged an increase in the Jewish birthrate on grounds which are essentially extra-theological. The calamitous losses of the Holocaust, coupled with defection as a result of assimilation and intermarriage, have decimated the Jewish population. If demographic trends are not reversed, it is argued, the prospects for Jewish survival are precarious. Thus, higher birthrates within the Jewish community must be encouraged if Jews are to remain a viable ethnic group capable of continuing the uniquely Jewish contribution to human civilization.

The question of whether or not non-Jews as well as Jews are bound by the commandment to "be fruitful and multiply" or by the more general injunction to "inhabit" the world as recorded by Isaiah is a subject of controversy among rabbinic authorities. Procreation is not enumerated among the seven commandments of the Noachide Code which Judaism views as binding upon non-Jews. Nevertheless, a leading eighth-century authority, R. Hai Gaon, affirms the universal applicability of this commandment. This is the view of the thirteenth-century Provencal talmudic scholar, R. Menachem ben Solomon Me'iri, and of some of the medieval French Tosafists as well. In modern times, this position was endorsed by R. Naftali Berlin, nineteenth-century head of the famed rabbinical academy of Volozhin. Other scholars, ranging from the thirteenth-century Spanish authority, R. Solomon ben Abraham Aderet, to the twentieth-century Lithuanian decisor, R. Joseph Rosen of Dvinsk, maintain that a non-Jew, while not bound by the positive commandment regarding procreation, is, nonetheless, forbidden to engage in onanism. At least some of the Tosafists are of the opinion that non-Jews are not at all bound by the provisions of Jewish law with regard to both procreation and onanism.

Arukh ha-Shulchan, a frequently consulted contemporary compendium of Jewish law, expresses an intermediate position. According to this source, insofar as non-Jews are concerned the commandment concerning procreation does not constitute a personal obligation but is directed to mankind in general. The human species, rather than each individual human being, is bidden to "be fruitful and multiply." According to this latter view, population expansion for non-Jews is in the nature of a theological desideratum rather than an obligation binding upon the individual. It is of more than cursory interest that this position is virtually identical with the view concerning procreation formulated by the prominent Catholic philosopher and theologian, Thomas Aquinas. To be sure, Aquinas' exposition of this view is based upon the doctrine of natural law rather than upon rabbinic sources. It is, nevertheless, one of many instances in which Catholic teaching differs from Jewish teaching as the latter pertains to members of the Jewish faith but is in conformity with Jewish tradition regarding the obligations of non-Jews who are bound by the provisions of the Noachide Code. It may well be argued that these similarities reflect the persistence of a "Noachide tradition" among adherents of Christianity long after the origin of that tradition was forgotten.

10

Contraception

Judaism recognizes sexuality as being natural to the human state. The sexual instinct may not, however, be given free reign. Channeled in the proper manner, viz., as intercourse between lawfully wedded husband and wife, it is not merely sanctioned but sanctified. Undoubtedly, mankind was endowed with sexual desire in order to assure procreation. Yet marriage, and the marital act, is sanctified even when it is known with certainty that the union will not be blessed with progeny. Jewish law explicitly recognizes other values inherent in sexual expression, and indeed ascribes to it a positive role in preserving both physical and mental health. Even more significant is the elevation of the marital act to the status of a *mitzvah* in its own right, quite apart from its instrumental necessity for propagation. The Torah, in defining the *mitzvah* of *onah* as a right which the wife may anticipate as her due, testifies to the role of sexuality in establishing the unique bonds formed between husband and wife and endows this relationship with holiness.

Recognition and sanctification of the multiple values inherent in the sexual act do not bestow the right to thwart its procreative role. It is the divine intention that all of these values be maximized. Frustration of procreative function, even while pursuing other wholly legitimate and even sacred goals is, in general, contrary to the divine will as reflected in Jewish law.

The prohibition against *hashchatat zera,* i.e. destruction of the male seed, serves as the basis of the stricture against most contraceptive measures, even when such practices are not designed to thwart fulfillment of the commandment to "be fruitful and multiply" (i.e., the couple are already parents of a son and a daughter). The sole exception to the prohibition against destruction of the male seed recognized by normative Halakhah is a situation in which pregnancy would pose a hazard to the life of the mother. When pregnancy would endanger the life of the mother such contraceptive measures are permissible because of the overriding concern for preservation of life.

Even this exception is by no means universally recognized. The *locus classicus* which serves as the focal point of all discussions of birth control in rabbinic literature is the "*Baraita* of the Three Women." (A *Baraita* is a teaching of one or more of the *Tanna'im,* i.e., the contributors of the Mishnah, and is historically contemporaneous with the Mishnah but is not included in the Mishnah itself.) It is extremely difficult to understand the subtleties of the discussion in the responsa literature without a full grasp of the *Baraita* as seen through the conflicting interpretations of Rashi and *Tosafot.* The text of the *Baraita* reads as follows:

> Three [categories of] women may use an absorbent[1] in their marital intercourse:[2] a minor and an expectant and nursing mother. The minor,[3] because otherwise she might become pregnant and die. An expectant mother[4] because otherwise she might cause her fetus to degenerate into a sandal.[5] A nursing mother,[6] because otherwise she might have to wean her child (prematurely)[7] and this would result in his death. And what is [the age of such] a minor?[8] From the age of eleven years and one day to the age of twelve years and one day. One who is under,[9] or over this age[10] must carry on her marital intercourse in a normal manner; so R. Meir. But the Sages said: The one as well as the other carries on her marital intercourse in a normal manner, and mercy[11] will be vouchsafed from Heaven, for it is said in the Scriptures, the Lord preserveth the simple.[12] (*Yevamot* 12b, Soncino translation.)

The overwhelming majority of talmudic scholars see a twofold but interconnected divergence between the interpretations of Rashi and *Tosafot* in their respective commentaries: (1) According to Rashi, the words *meshamshot be-mokh* are to be understood as meaning that the three women *may* use a *mokh* or tampon. The Sages, in disagreeing with R. Meir, *forbid* the use of the *mokh.* (2) According to Rashi, the reference is to a precoital *mokh* or tampon. Since use of a precoital *mokh* clearly involves an act of *hashchatat zera,* its use is restricted by R. Meir to the "three women" whose lives would be endangered by pregnancy. Other women are certainly not permitted to use such devices. (Since the halakhic decision is in accordance with the opinion of the Sages, the "three women" would also not be permitted use of the *mokh* insofar as normative Halakhah is concerned.)

Rashi is silent with regard to use of a postcoital contraceptive device. The Tosafists disagree as to whether or not use of a postcoital device is objectionable according to Rashi. The pivotal question is whether or not women are bound by the prohibition concerning destruction of the male seed. If the answer is yes, there is no difference between a precoital and a postcoital *mokh.* A postcoital contraceptive inserted by the female partner after intercourse is thus no different, halakhically speaking, from the precoital insertion of a tampon. However, if women are not restricted in this manner, there exists no restraint upon the use of a postcoital tampon even by "other women" since the act of *hashchatah* is performed by the female. With the use of a precoital *mokh* the act of intercourse itself constitutes *hashchatat zera* on the part of the male.

Rabbenu Tam, one of the most prominent of the French Tosafists, differs with regard to both points: (1) He understands the *Baraita* to be discussing use of a postcoital *mokh* exclusively. Since, according to Rabbenu Tam, women are not restricted with regard to *hashchatat zera,* there is no objection to use of a postcoital device by any woman. (2) Accordingly, R. Meir could not simply be expressing permissibility insofar as the "three women" are concerned, because the act in question is never objectionable. Therefore, Rabbenu Tam, as cited by *Tosafot,* interprets the term *meshamshot* as meaning that the "three women" are *required* to use the *mokh.* R. Meir is thus understood as stating that women have no right to assume the risk of hazardous pregnancy. The Sages disagree and permit, but do not require, the "three women" to hazard this risk. For Rabbenu Tam, even the "three women" are forbidden use of a precoital device, even according to the more liberal opinion of R. Meir.

The halakhic ruling to be derived from this analysis is that use of a precoital device is absolutely forbidden even for the "three women." According to *Tosafot,* it is equally forbidden by the Sages and R. Meir; for Rashi it is forbidden by the authoritative position of the Sages. This is indeed the conclusion reached by R. Akiva Eger,[13] R. Moses Sofer (late 18th and early 19th cents.),[14] and R. Ya'akov Ettlinger (19th cent.).[15] The situation with regard to a postcoital device is less clear-cut. Here the crucial question is whether Rabbenu Tam's lenient view may be adopted despite the reservations voiced by Ri, another of the Tosafists. R. Moses Sofer accepts the permissive view. R. Akiva Eger marshals evidence to show that the majority of early authorities made no distinction between precoital and postcoital devices and interprets the position of the Sages as forbidding both devices even in cases of danger. Rabbi Akiva Eger sanctions use of a postcoital tampon only when it will do no good, i.e., for the absorption of semen remaining in the vaginal tract which will not fertilize the ovum.

This position is modified by some authorities, notably by the renowned early twentieth-century authority, R. Chaim Ozer Grodzinski of Vilna, who maintains that the disagreement of the *Baraita* is limited to the relatively low risk incurred by the "three women," but that in the case of a clear hazard the Sages would concur in permitting even precoital contraception.[16] (Some scholars maintain that even R. Akiva Eger did not intend to restrict the use of a precoital tampon in cases of clear-cut danger.[17] It is, however, difficult to read this meaning into R. Akiva Eger's comments.) It is this latter view which is followed by most contemporary rabbinic decisors.[18]

One significant point must be underscored. This is not a situation in which halakhic proscriptions are suspended due to considerations of *pikuach nefesh* (danger to life). Halakhah is suspended only when there is no other way of avoiding danger. In the case of the "three women" there are other alternatives, albeit harsh ones: abstinence or divorce. Use of precoital contraceptive devices is permitted, not on the basis of danger to life *per se,* but on the basis of the rationale that no violation of *hashchatat zera* occurs because such intercourse is "normal" in the case of a woman to whom pregnancy poses a danger to life.

The prohibition against *hotza'at zera le-vatalah* is a prohibition against emission of semen "in vain." Proper definition of the term "in vain" is crucial for establishing the parameters of the prohibition. Were all ejaculation other than for purposes of procreation deemed to be in vain, it would follow that any act of sexual intercourse which could not result in pregnancy would be prohibited as constituting an emission of semen "in vain." The implication of such an erroneous position would be that cohabitation with an infertile woman or with a woman who has experienced menopause would be forbidden. This, of course, is not the case. Judaism does not frown upon the marriage of a sterile or post-menopausal woman, provided that the male partner has fulfilled his obligation with regard to procreation.

Tosafot, in formulating the definition of the concept "in vain," explains that ejaculation as the culmination of normal sexual intercourse can never be deemed "in vain." This may be understood in light of the fact that Judaism, as distinct from some other religious systems, does not view propagation of the species as the sole purpose and justification of sexual intercourse. Judaism posits *onah* (marital relations) as an obligation which devolves upon the husband. The essence of this obligation is the duty of the husband to provide for the sexual gratification of his wife. Claim for fulfillment of this obligation is the legal right of the wife no less than her right to be provided with food and clothing. The nature and extent of this obligation is underscored in the statement of one authority who counsels that a wife should perform the monthly immersion in a ritualarium even if the couple cannot engage in intercourse. Even in such circumstances the husband is obligated to initiate other forms of physical intimacy for the gratification of his wife.[19] Accordingly, intercourse with a woman who is incapable of bearing children does not constitute emission of semen "in vain" provided that there is no attempt to "waste" or destroy the seed.

The use of a tampon or similar contraceptive device when pregnancy poses a danger to the life of the female partner is sanctioned by numerous authorities on the basis of the rationale that (1) the emission of semen is not in vain since it is designed to fulfill the licit purpose of gratifying the female spouse, and (2) no "waste" is involved since the woman has no right, much less an obligation, to place her life in danger by becoming pregnant. A similar but somewhat modified formulation of this rationale is advanced by other authorities who stress that intercourse with a barren partner is not prohibited because the sexual act is performed in a normal or usual manner "in accordance with the way of the entire world." Use of a tampon, even if the woman is incapable of conceiving a child, is not usual or natural. However, since a woman for whom pregnancy poses a life-threatening danger does not normally cohabit in any other way, use of a tampon is deemed to be normal and usual under such circumstances.

Since intercourse must be conducted in as "usual" a manner as possible, it may be readily understood that a diaphragm is to be preferred over a condom as a means of eliminating a threat of the life of the female partner. Some authorities are indeed prepared to sanction a condom as well when pregnancy would pose a danger to the life of the mother, since its use does not necessarily impede gratification of the female partner.[20] Others, however, maintain that the condom should not be viewed as the preferred method of contraception because of the attendant unnatural quality of the sexual act.[21]

As has been indicated, use of a diaphragm is limited to situations in which pregnancy would endanger the life of the female partner. Under less drastic conditions, the physical barrier which prevents the semen from entering the cervix constitutes "destruction" of the male seed. There are, indeed, other contraceptives which serve to prevent pregnancy from occurring but do not involve destruction of the seed. Such measures, while not tantamount to onanism, are contraindicated by virtue of the obligation to "be fruitful and multiply" and by virtue of man's obligation with regard to *shevet* (populating the universe). The latter obligation is not, however, so overriding in nature that it must be fulfilled even at the cost of compromising the health of the mother. Accordingly, an examination of available contraceptive measures is in order, with the understanding that employment of such measures may be considered only upon prior presentation of the pertinent medical considerations to a competent rabbinic authority for halakhic determination that avoidance of pregnancy is permissible.

Some authorities have argued that spermicides do not constitute "destruction" of the seed in the halakhic sense of the term.[22] Mechanical contraceptives, such as the tampon or the diaphragm, prevent conception by means of interposing a physical barrier which has the effect of preventing contact between the sperm and the ovum, and hence "destroys" the seed. Spermicides are designed to render the sperm impotent so that conception does not result even when contact is achieved. The changes which occur to the sperm are chemical in nature and cannot be perceived by the naked eye. Halakhah is usually not concerned with phenomena not readily perceivable by the sensory organs. Hence, even in face of the biblical prohibition against eating "creeping things," there is no objection to drinking a glass of water, despite the presence in the water of vast numbers of microbes. Since the presence of germs can be detected only by means of a microscope, they are "non-existent" insofar as Jewish law is concerned. These authorities argue that chemical changes designed to destroy the virility of the sperm are not to be equated with "destruction" of the seed. Others, rejecting this view, maintain that the resultant infertility of the sperm is a readily ascertainable phenomenon and, hence, utilization of a spermicide constitutes an act of destruction. Moreover, many spermicides, vaginal foams in particular, have a twofold effect. In addition to destroying the virility of the sperm, they are designed to produce an occlusion in the form of a foam which serves to prevent the free passage of the sperm through the genital tract. The latter effect is tantamount to the introduction of a mechanical barrier which constitutes an act of destruction.

Assessment of intrauterine devices (I.U.D.) is impeded by the fact that medical science does not fully understand the mechanism which prevents pregnancy. Were it the case that conception does not occur because the sperm is somehow inhibited from penetrating the ovum, but without the potency of the sperm being destroyed, the I.U.D. would be a preferred method of contraception when birth control is advisable. There is, however, some evidence that the I.U.D. functions as an abortifacient or, even more likely, that it interferes with implantation of the fertilized ovum in the wall of the uterus.[23] On the other hand, those authorities who sanction abortion during the earliest stages of gestation for considerations of maternal health would certainly permit the use of an I.U.D. in such circumstances.

The nylon cord attached to the I.U.D. presents a further complication. Some authorities question whether the nylon cord does not constitute a *chatzitzah* or foreign object upon the body which interferes with the monthly immersion in a ritualarium; others see no problem, provided that the cord is short and does not descend much below the cervical os, since it is in a place deep within the body. Another problem is perceived by some scholars who maintain that the cord introduces an "unnatural" quality if it can be felt by the male. It further seems to present a partial barrier to the free flow of semen in the genital tract. Strictly speaking, the cord does not serve a medical purpose. It is designed to facilitate removal of the I.U.D. and also serves to assure the wearer that it has not, in fact, been expelled by the body. The cord may, therefore, be detached without ill effect. The contraceptive effect of the I.U.D. is undiminished if the cord is removed prior to insertion.

A practical complication with regard to use of the I.U.D. is the fact that it may cause staining or spotting, particularly during the early months of use, as a result of uterine contractions. Such bleeding poses a serious problem with regard to marital relations, as will be discussed shortly. These contractions may also lead to perforations of the uterus and other medical complications. For these reasons, both competent medical and rabbinic advice should be sought prior to use of an I.U.D.

Oral contraception by use of a pill is, at least in theory, the least objectionable method of birth control. The pill contains hormones similar to those which are secreted by the body during pregnancy. These hormones have the effect of suppressing ovulation, thereby preventing the superimposition of a new pregnancy upon an already pregnant woman. The effect of the pill is to simulate the physiological state associated with pregnancy and thereby to prevent ovulation from occurring.

This method of contraception is akin to the "cup of roots" which was known in the time of the Gemara. *Yevamot* 65b reports that the wife of R. Chiyya, having suffered an agonizing childbirth, was authorized to imbibe such a potion. The "cup of roots" mentioned in the Gemara seems to have caused permanent sterility and, hence, according to some authorities, could be used only in extreme situations. Since the effect of the pill is temporary, it does not pose a similar problem. This method, of course, involves no question of destruction of the seed and, hence, would be the preferred method when contraception is warranted.

Use of the pill does, however, pose a problem unassociated with birth control. The pill may cause intramenstrual staining or spotting. While it is of no medical significance, such bleeding does signify a state of *niddah.* Since sexual relations between husband and wife are precluded by virtue of the laws of *niddah,* use of a birth-control measure which has this effect is self-defeating. It is for this reason that prominent halakhic authorities voiced objections to use of the pill when it was first introduced. In recent years oral contraceptives have been perfected and now contain lesser dosages of hormones. It is reported that with the use of present hormone dosages the percentage of women who experience intramenstrual bleeding is considerably lower than in the past. Moreover, intramenstrual bleeding, even when experienced initially, may cease within a relatively short period of time. When the pill is sanctioned as a contraceptive measure, a tampon should be utilized at least during the first month of use in order to determine that staining has not occurred.

It should also be noted that there are serious medical problems associated with use of the pill. Particularly when taken over a long period of time, the pill may be carcinogenic in nature. While at least for some women the risk of pregnancy may be greater than the risk associated with the pill, women who use the pill do experience a higher statistical incidence of strokes, particularly when there is a history of cardiovascular disease. Moreover, many gynecologists now advise against pregnancy for a period of three months following termination of use of the pill because of fear of possible genetic defects. For all of these reasons, competent medical and rabbinic advice should be sought in each individual case.

NOTES

1. *Mokh:* "hackled wool or flax."
2. To prevent contraception.
3. Is permitted the use of an absorbent.

4. Is permitted the use of an absorbent.

5. Sandal, lit., "a flat fish"; a fish-shaped abortion due to superfetation.

6. Is permitted the use of an absorbent.

7. On account of her second conception, which causes the deterioration of her breast milk.

8. Who is capable of conception, but is exposed thereby to danger.

9. When no conception is possible.

10. When pregnancy involves no fatal consequence.

11. To protect her from danger.

12. Psalms 116:6; those who are unable to protect themselves.

13. *Teshuvot R. Akiva Eger,* no. 71.

14. *Teshuvot Chatam Sofer, Yoreh De'ah,* no. 172.

15. *Teshuvot Binyan Zion,* no. 137.

16. *Teshuvot Achi'ezer, Even ha-Ezer,* no. 23.

17. *Chazon Ish, Even ha-Ezer* 37:5; R. Moshe Feinstein, *Iggrot Mosheh, Even ha-Ezer,* I, no. 63, p. 159.

18. See *Otzar ha-Poskim,* IX, 206.

19. *Teshuvot Even Shoham,* no. 14; *Pitchei Teshuvah, Yoreh De'ah* 184:22; cf. however, *Arukh ha-Shulchan* 184:43. See also *Chokhmat Adam* 108:7.

20. *Teshuvot Achiezer,* III, no. 24.

21. See *Iggrot Mosheh, Even ha-Ezer,* II, no. 63, and *Otzar ha-Poskim,* IX, 227 ff.

22. See *Iggrot Mosheh, Even ha-Ezer,* I, no. 65, and *Otzar ha-Poskim,* IX, 229 ff.

23. Assuming this to be the case, some authorities permit use of an I.U.D. for reasons of maternal health on the grounds that in such a situation measures need not be taken to preserve the fetus.

11

Sterilization

The Gemara, *Shabbat* 110b, derives a prohibition against castration of both male human beings and male animals from the verse, "And that which is mauled or crushed or torn or cut you shall not offer unto the Lord; nor should you do this in your land" (Leviticus 22:24). This verse is understood by the Gemara as having reference to the male sexual organs and hence the latter part of the verse constitutes a prohibition against emasculation. Accordingly, an orchidectomy, i.e., surgical removal of the testicles, may be performed only if necessary to alleviate a life-threatening situation, e.g., carcinoma of the prostate gland. For this reason, vasectomy is not acceptable as a form of contraception or for purposes of eugenic sterilization.

The prohibition against sterilization gives rise to the need for a possible modification of the procedure to be followed in prostate surgery. It is the practice of many urologists to sever the vas deferens when performing a prostatectomy. Although this does not render the patient impotent it does leave him sterile. When there is indeed serious medical need for cutting the vas deferens this should, of course, be done.[1] However, this procedure should not be carried out simply as a matter of routine. In the past this was done routinely as a precautionary measure in order to avoid an infection known as epididymitis. Recent studies, however, show that this procedure is unnecessary and of little or no effect.[2] As a result, a number of major medical centers have abandoned this practice. In some hospitals antibiotics are administered prophylactically in order to accomplish the same result.[3] In other hospitals even this is considered to be superfluous.

Sterilization of the female is also ordinarily forbidden by Jewish law. *Tosafot* and Rashba, in their respective commentaries on *Shabbat* 111a, indicate that this prohibition is limited to removal of male sexual organs and that there exists no biblical prohibition with regard to sterilization of a female. The terminology employed by Maimonides (*Issurei Bi'ah* 16:11) and *Shulchan Arukh* (*Even ha-Ezer* 5:11) would seem to indicate that the position of the latter authorities is that surgical sterilization of women, while not an actionable offense, is nevertheless biblically proscribed. Although the reference in Leviticus 22:24 is limited to external male organs, R. Elijah of Vilna[4] cites *Sifra* in explaining that the ban against removal of the internal female sexual organs is derived from the formulation employed in the very next verse, Leviticus 22:25. Nevertheless, other authorities[5] maintain that, even according to Maimonides, the prohibition against sterilization of females is rabbinic in nature. Once decisor[6] goes beyond the position of other authorities in averring that there is no prohibition with regard to female sterilization *per se* but that it is nonetheless forbidden to subject female animals to this procedure because of the general prohibition against causing pain to animals. Similarly, nontherapeutic sterilization of women would constitute an unlawful act of "wounding"—*chavalah.*

The question of sterilization of a mentally incompetent woman who might be subject to sexual abuse is discussed in a number of rabbinic responsa. It should be stressed that neither mental incompetence *per se* nor eugenic considerations are significant factors in terms of a halakhic ruling with regard to this issue.

Some authorities are inclined to permit sterilization when pregnancy would pose a threat to the health of the mother but stipulate that the surgical procedure should be performed by a non-Jewish medical practitioner. *Shulchan Arukh, Even ha-Ezer* 5:11, expressly declares that a non-Jew may not be requested to castrate an animal belonging to a Jew. Nevertheless, these decisors permit sterilization to be performed by a non-Jewish physician in order to preserve the health of the woman. Some authorities assert that all rabbinic prohibitions are suspended with regard to matters affecting human health even if no threat to life is involved. Employing this principle, it is argued that, according to those authorities who maintain that female sterilization is banned only by reason of rabbinic edict, the procedure in question could be performed even by a Jewish physician. There are, however, numerous authorities who are of the opinion that sterilization of women is forbidden by biblical law. Moreover, even those rabbinic scholars who maintain that the sterilization of women is itself biblically forbidden recognize that the prohibition against requesting a non-Jew to perform the action in question is rabbinic in nature. Hence, it is argued, even if the ban against requesting a non-Jew to perform sterilization encompasses sterilization of females, which is itself a matter of some doubt, the prohibition is suspended if the procedure is indicated for therapeutic reasons. Accordingly, these authorities rule that a non-Jewish surgeon may be engaged to render this service.

Other contemporary rabbinic authorities rule that not all rabbinic prohibitions are suspended for reasons of health. Hence, they argue, even according to those authorities who maintain that the prohibition against sterilization of a female is rabbinic in nature, sterilization for therapeutic purposes cannot be sanctioned unless pregnancy poses a threat to the life of the mother.

NOTES

1. For a discussion of the halakhic issues involved see *Chazon Ish, Even ha-Ezer* 12:7; R. Iser Yehudah Unterman, *Otzar ha-Poskim,* I (3rd edition, 5711), *he'arot,* pp. 326–329; R. Ya'akov Breisch, *Chelkat Ya'akov,* II, no. 22; R. Yitzchak Ya'akov Weisz, Minchat Yitzchok, II, no. 123, sec. 6; R. Eliezer Waldenberg, Tzitz Eliezer, X, no. 25, Chap. 24; R. Nisan Telushkin, *Ha-Pardes,* Iyar 5715; Dr. Israel Baruch Ness, *Ha-Pardes,* Nisan 5716 and *Ha-Pardes,* Cheshvan 5731; R. Menachem Schneersohn, *Ha-Ma'or,* Tammuz 5725; R. Ephraim Yolles, *Ha-Ma'or,* Tevet 5731; R. Baruch Mordecai Birg, *No'am,* I (5718), 245–262; R. Moshe Feinstein, *Le-Torah ve-Hora'ah,* no. 5 (Shevu'ot 5735), pp. 18–19; and *Otzrot Yerushalayim,* no. 297 (5732).

2. Jack M. Lynn and Reed M. Nesbit, "The Influence of Vasectomy upon the Incidence of Epididymitis Following Transurethral Prostatectomy," *Journal of Urology,* vol 59, no. 1 (January 1948), pp. 72–75; and George Haralambidis and Anthony N. Spinelli, "Vasectomy: An Evaluation," *Journal of Urology,* vol. 89, no. 4 (April 1963), pp. 591–594.

3. James J. Plorde *et al.,* "Course and Prognosis of Prostatectomy;

With a Note on the Incidence of Bacteremia and Effectiveness of Chemoprophylaxis," *New England Journal of Medicine,* vol. 272, no. 6 (February 11, 1965), pp. 269–277.

4. *Bi'ur ha-Gra, Even ha-Ezer* 5:25–26.
5. *Chatam Sofer, Even ha-Ezer* 5:22.
6. *Turei Zahav, Even ha-Ezer* 5:6.

12

Homosexuality

The Bible specifically prohibits homosexual acts between males and, of all sexual perversions, singles out homosexual activity as an act of *to'evah*—an "abomination." "You shall not lie with a man as one lies with a woman; it is an abomination" (Leviticus 18:22). Homosexual acts are among those forms of sexual licentiousness which constitute a cardinal sin for which a Jew must sacrifice his life rather than transgress. Lesbianism is included in the biblical admonition[1] against participation in deviant sexual practices associated with the Egyptians and Canaanites of antiquity (Leviticus 18:3), but is not a capital offense. The ultimate crime of the city of Sodom and the transgression upon which its fate was sealed was the attempted homosexual rape of the two strangers who, unknown to the townspeople, were angels of God. The entire population of the city surrounded the home of Lot and demanded that he surrender his guests to them "that we may know them" (Genesis 19:5). The verb "to know" is the biblical euphemism for the sexual act. This narrative is the basis for the introduction of the term "sodomy" into the English language as a synonym for male homosexuality.

Biblical commandments and proscriptions are endowed with eternal validity by virtue of their status as the revealed will of God. Nevertheless, man is permitted, and even encouraged, to endeavor to comprehend, insofar as he is capable, the elements of divine wisdom which are reflected in God's commandments. Accordingly, Jewish scholars, over the course of millennia, have endeavored to formulate the considerations and goals reflected in the various *mitzvot,* but always with a clear awareness that, since man cannot plumb the depths of divine wisdom, any humanly perceived rationale cannot be exhaustive in nature. Hence, any such explanation, while enabling us to acquire a philosophical perspective with regard to observance of specific commandments, has no bearing upon the formulation of Jewish law. Reasons offered in understanding the purpose of *mitzvot* can in no way modify the halakhah governing actual practice.

The term *to'evah* (lit. "abomination") is rendered by talmudic exegesis as "*to'eh attach bah*—you go astray by virtue of it." The precise nature of "going astray" by virtue of homosexuality is the subject of varying interpretations. *Sefer ha-Chinnukh* explains that man is charged with populating the universe. Through procreation man assists in fulfillment of the divine plan of creation. Homosexual activity frustrates fulfillment of this goal.

Tosafot and *Rosh, Nedarim* 51a, indicate that the homosexual goes astray in the sense that he abandons his family. According to this interpretation, the abomination associated with such conduct lies in the destruction of the family unit. The homosexual cannot lead a normal family life. Parenthetically, homosexuality was prevalent in ancient civilizations and this fact was well known to the Sages of the Talmud. However, the Talmud, in enumerating the relatively few meritorious practices of pagan societies of old, praises them because "they do not write a marriage contract for a male," i.e., they did not attempt to present "homosexual marriage" as an acceptable alternative to heterosexual marriage.

One should be aware of the distinction between homosexuality and homosexual conduct. Some individuals are sexually attracted to members of their own sex but feel no similar attraction to members of the opposite sex. This deeply felt attraction may or may not find expression in overt sexual activity. Persons afflicted in this manner are homosexuals even if they remain celibate or engage in heterosexual activity exclusively. Whether such a condition is to be regarded as a pathology or as a normal sexual interest is of little practical significance. There is indeed strong reason to believe that Judaism regards homosexuality (as distinct from homosexual conduct) as pathological. If homosexuality is an aberration, then, of course, a cure must be attempted. Yet, even if the tendency is not associated with some form of mental illness but is consistent with a well-integrated personality, it must be recognized that this tendency may not be acted upon because homosexual conduct is forbidden. Thus, Jewish teaching would require that the homosexual seek psychiatric help designed to overcome this tendency so that he may be enabled to lead a healthy and satisfying life as a heterosexual.

The homosexual act is a matter quite distinct from the state of homosexuality. The former is an act governed by free will, while the latter is a state of being. The former can be proscribed; the latter may well be beyond a person's control. It is the act, rather than the psychological state, which is the subject of the Torah's admonition.

Performance of homosexual acts is not limited to homosexuals. A heterosexual may engage in a homosexual act because a partner of the opposite gender is unavailable, because of a desire to enjoy varied and diverse sexual pleasures, or simply out of a desire to partake of forbidden fruits. In its most fundamental sense, the prohibition against homosexual conduct serves to teach that such acts, even when performed by consenting adults, are not morally neutral and hence unobjectionable, but constitute an odious abomination. Given this perspective with regard to the nature of the act, it follows that persons afflicted with homosexual tendencies must be aided in overcoming their unnatural desires. Psychiatric treatment, in particular, should be undertaken with a view to enabling the patient to overcome homosexual tendencies rather than for the purpose of confirming and integrating such behavior.

While Judaism regards the homosexual act with repugnance, it has the greatest sympathy for the homosexual as a person, as distinct from its attitude toward the heterosexual who engages in homosexual activity purely for the sake of sexual gratification. The homosexual must be given sympathetic consideration and support in his attempt to overcome his condition. This does not mean that Judaism can be supportive of continued homosexual activity even on the part of a manifestly pathological homosexual. If indeed there are homosexuals who literally cannot control their actions—and this is regarded by most psychiatrists as highly unlikely—their status, insofar as culpability is concerned, is analogous to that of a person who goes berserk and embarks upon a rampage of crime. Such a person is in the category of an *onus* (the Hebrew term for a person acting as a result of a *force majeure*)—an individual deprived of *bechirah,* or the ability to exercise free will, by virtue of his pathological condition. No person can be held responsible for an act over which he has no control. However, most, and probably all, homosexuals can curb these actions, albeit at times only with extreme difficulty. Psychiatrists have an obligation not only to correct the underlying pathology but also to assist their patients in refraining from overt acts of a homosexual nature. It is estimated that as many as a third of all homosexuals may ultimately be cured, and it is believed that with utilization of psychiatric behavior-control techniques the rate of success is even higher.

Society has a definite obligation not to bestow a seal of legitimacy upon homosexual activity. Rabbi Isaac Arama, in his philosophical commentary on the Bible, points out that the homosexual conduct of Sodom was punished with much more severity than the homosexuality which was rampant in other societies. The reason, he explains, is because in Sodom homosexuality was ritualized: "The people of Sodom agreed among themselves that any stranger entering the city would be subjected to homosexual intercourse." Removal of the odium associated with a transgression is even more serious a matter than the transgression itself.

The question of imposition by the state of penal sanctions for homosexual violations is beyond the scope of this discussion. It may be cogently argued that such penalties are, in practice, not mandated by Jewish law and are indeed counter-productive. However, in codifying the obligation of the Sons of Noah, i.e., gentiles, with regard to the commandment concerning *dinin,* the last of the Seven Noachide Commandments, Maimonides declares that this commandment imposes two distinct obligations: (1) to establish a judicial system for purposes of meting out punishment for violation of the first six commandments; and (2) the appointment of judges "to admonish the people." Irrespective of its obligation to punish violators, society has an obligation to admonish, i.e., to enact legislation designed to serve as an admonition. The admonition is, in itself, a matter of positive moral value in that it serves to discourage homosexual activity. Moreover, such legislation, whether or not it is subsequently enforced, signifies society's disapproval and moral condemnation.

NOTES

1. *Sifra* 9:8; *Kiryat Sefer, Hilkhot Issurei Bi'ah,* chap. 21.

13

Transsexual Surgery and Ambiguous Genitalia

Transsexuals are persons born with the anatomy of one sex but who suffer from an identification with the other sex which in many instances is total and lifelong. It is claimed by some scientists doing research in this area that this abnormality is the result of homone disturbances which are quite likely prenatal in origin. In a rapidly increasing number of cases, transsexualism is now being treated medically by a combination of hormone therapy and sex-change surgery. While such operations were performed in Europe on an intermittent basis as early as 1930, sex-change operations have become prevalent in our country only since the late 1960's. There are an estimated ten thousand transsexuals in the United States, of whom approximately fifteen hundred have changed their sex by means of surgery. Public awareness of this phenomenon has been heightened in recent years as a result of the publication of *Conundrum,* an autobiography by Jan (formerly James) Morris, in which the author discusses his own transsexualism with skill and sensitivity.

Despite earlier enthusiasm on the part of some psychiatrists for sex-change surgery as a treatment for transsexualism, psychiatric studies now indicate that such surgery is of little effect in improving the condition of transsexuals. Two prominent psychiatrists recently completed an evaluation of the family relationships, general stability, and adaptability to daily routine of a number of former patients who had undergone sex-change operations. This study discovered no significant difference in adjustment between those who were treated by means of sex-reversal surgery and those who were not treated surgically.[1]

Sex-change operations involving the surgical removal of sexual organs are clearly forbidden on the basis of the explicit biblical prohibition, "And that which is mauled or crushed or torn or cut you shall not offer unto the Lord; nor should you do this in your land" (Leviticus 22:24). Sterilization of women is also prohibited, as recorded in *Even ha-Ezer* 5:11.

One authority[2] notes that yet another prohibition is also applicable to sex-change procedures, a consideration which may extend as well to hormone treatment for purposes of sex-change. The commandment "A woman shall not wear that which pertains to a man, nor shall a man put on a woman's garment" (Deuteronomy 22:5) is not limited to the wearing of apparel associated with the opposite sex but encompasses any action uniquely identified with the opposite sex, proscribing, for example, shaving of armpits or dyeing of hair by a male. A procedure designed to transform sexual characteristics violates the very essence of this prohibition.

Once a sexual transformation has actually been effected, a host of practical halakhic questions arise. The resolution of these questions hinges upon the crucial conceptual problem of whether or not a change of sex has indeed occurred from the point of view of Halakhah. It should be emphasized that while sexual organs can be removed, medical science is (at least as yet) incapable of substituting functional reproductive organs of the opposite sex. Sex-change procedures involve the construction of stimulated sexual organs devoid of reproductive powers.

The most obvious halakhic questions concern the sexual status of such individuals with regard to marriage and divorce, and with regard to their status vis-à-vis the respective obligations of men and women in the performance of *mitzvot. Teshuvot Besamim Rosh,*[3] no. 130, questions whether a man whose genitalia have been completely removed need divorce his wife in order to dissolve their marriage or whether a divorce is unnecessary since the male has been sexually transformed and hence "a new body has appeared and is comparable to a woman's." *Besamim Rosh* reaches no definitive conclusion with regard to whether or not a divorce is necessary in the event that the operation is performed subsequent to entry into a valid marriage. However, *Besamim Rosh* strongly asserts that, regardless of an individual's sexual status with regard to other matters, once the male sexual organs have been removed the person in question is no longer competent to contract a valid marriage as a man. Although not stated explicitly, it may be assumed that, according to *Besamim Rosh,* such a person is also unqualified to contract a marriage as a woman since true female genital organs remain lacking even subsequent to successful completion of the surgical procedure.

For *Besamin Rosh* sexual identity insofar as marriage is concerned depends entirely upon the presence of genital organs. No mention is made of the presence or absence of secondary sexual characteristics and, indeed, it is not difficult to understand why they are deemed irrelevant. There is no evidence that the transformation of secondary sexual characteristics affects sexual status in any way, insofar as Jewish law is concerned.

There is at least one source which apparently declares that a male cannot acquire the status of a woman by means of surgery. Rabbenu Chananel, quoted by Ibn Ezra in his commentary on Leviticus 18:22, declares that intercourse between a normal male and a male in whom artifical female sexual organs have been fashioned by means of surgery constitutes sodomy. This would appear to be the case, according to Rabbenu Chananel, even if the male genitalia are removed.

The corollary to this question arises with regard to a woman who has acquired the sexual characteristics of a male as a result of transsexual surgery. A nineteenth-century author, Rabbi Yosef Palaggi, *Yosef et Echav* 3:5, opines that no divorce is necessary in order to dissolve a marriage contracted prior to such transformation. This author goes beyond the position of *Besamim Rosh* who, as noted, did not reach a definitive conclusion in his discussion of the parallel question with regard to sex change in a male. In opposition to Rabbi Palaggi's view it may, however, be argued that gender is irreversibly determined at birth and that sex, insofar as Halakhah is concerned, cannot be transformed by surgical procedures. This position is particularly cogent in view of the fact that fertile organs of the opposite sex cannot be acquired by means of surgery. The view that sexual identity cannot be changed by means of surgery would appear to be the position of Rabbenu Chananel. According to Rabbenu Chananel, this principle would appear to govern all halakhic questions pertaining to sexual identity.

Parenthetically, it is of interest to note that various courts in the United States have ruled that, in the eyes of the law, surgery to transform genitalia has no effect upon the gender of the person upon whom such procedures are performed.[4] Recently, a justice of the New York State Supreme Court ruled that a woman who underwent surgery to become a man and subsequently married could not seek a divorce since a valid marriage had, in fact, never existed. The decision states that a marriage contract entered into by individuals of the same sex, one of whom has undergone sex-reversal surgery, has no validity, either in fact or in law.[5]

Another interesting question arises with regard to circumcision. In female-to-male transformations a simulated male organ is often created by means of skin grafts and silicone forms. In some cases this effect is achieved by freeing the clitoris from its connective tissue. There is no question that this newly fashioned organ need not be circumcised. This is abundantly clear from the conclusion reached by *She'ilat Ya'avetz,* I, no. 171, in the course of his discussion of a similar question arising with regard to a congenital defect. Circumcision would be unnecessary even if the new organ were physiologically similar to that of a male in every respect. In the opinion of this authority, the phraseology employed by Scripture, "uncircumcised male" (Genesis 17:13), applies solely to an individual who is a male at the time of birth.

Although Judaism does not sanction reversal of sex by means of surgery, transsexualism is a disorder which should receive the fullest measure of medical and psychiatric treatment consistent with Halakhah. Transsexuals should be encouraged to undergo treatment to correct endocrine imbalances, when medically indicated, and to seek psychiatric guidance in order to alleviate the grave emotional problems which are frequently associated with this tragic condition.

The gender of a transsexual before sex-reversal therapy is undertaken is not at all in doubt. Although the individual may experience grave psychological trauma, a positive determination of sex may be made on the basis of clear anatomical identification with one sex or the other. In sharp contrast, the determination of the sex of an infant born with ambiguous genitalia is fraught with difficulty. The child may be either male, female or a hermaphrodite. The most frequently observable sign of ambiguous gender is the presence of an organ which may be either a malformed penis or an enlarged clitoris.

There is an understandable desire on the part of many physicians to consider such infants females and to perform whatever surgical procedures may be necessary to simulate the anatomy of a female. The considerations motivating such a course of treatment are psychological in nature. There is a clear psychological need for unequivocal sexual identification. Medically speaking, it is much easier to enable the child to develop and to function as a female than as a male. Inability to function sexually as a male cannot at present be overcome by means of medical treatment. The child may, however, be enabled to funtion as a female much more readily, even though sterility may not be overcome.

Jewish law does not sanction sex determination on the basis of psychological considerations. The presence of testes, either external or internal, is an absolute indication that the child is not a female, although other criteria may lead to a determination of hermaphroditism. Surgical removal of the testes constitutes an act of castration which is forbidden by Leviticus 22:24. Neither the desire to rear the child as a female nor the child's future inability to function as a male in sexual relations is sufficient reason to remove the testes. They may, however, be removed if failure to do so presents a possible hazard to the life of the child, e.g., possible carcinoma. Surgical removal for therapeutic reasons does not, however, effect a halakhic change of sexual status.

Moreover, both surgical and hormonal modification of gender may pose grave problems with regard to possible homosexual activity later in life. For this reason, as well as for determination of sex insofar as other aspects of Halakhah are concerned, every decision with regard to the grave and often pain-fraught problems of sex determination requires consultation with competent rabbinic authorities.

NOTES

1. Jon K. Meyer and Donna J. Retter, "Sex Reassignment," *Archives of General Psychiatry,* XXXVI (August 1979), 1010–1015.

2. Rabbi Meir Amsel, *Ha-Ma'or,* Kislev–Tevet 5733.

3. *Teshuvot Besamim Rosh* is commonly attributed to Rabbenu Asher ben Yechiel, although the authenticity of this work is questioned by many.

4. *Anonymous v. Anonymous,* 67 Misc. 2d 982; *Baker v. Nelson,* 291 Minn. 310, 191 N.W. 2d 185; 409 U.S. 810, 93 Supreme Court, 37; *Jones v. Hallahan,* Ky., 501 S.W. 2d 588.

5. *New York Law Journal,* April 30, 1974, p. 17, col. 4.

14

Artificial Insemination

A host of legal and ethical problems are posed by A.I.D. (artificial insemination utilizing donor semen). It is important to recognize that these problems are separable into categories: (1) the permissibility of the procedure itself; (2) *post-factum* questions which arise with regard to paternity, consanguinity, rights of inheritance, fulfillment of the commandment with regard to procreation insofar as the donor is concerned, etc. The latter do not affect the permissibility of the procedure *per se;* they simply pose questions which must be resolved when A.I.D., whether permissible or not, has occurred.

It is recognized by all rabbinic authorities that there are no religious or ethical grounds which augur in favor of encouraging the practice of artificial insemination utilizing donor semen. The most usual reason for employment of A.I.D. is infertility of the husband and his consequent inability to impregnate his wife. Jewish law recognizes no relationship whatsoever between the husband of a woman so impregnated and the child born as a result of A.I.D. Quite obviously, a husband incapable of siring a child cannot fulfill the commandment to "be fruitful and multiply." The husband fulfills no *mitzvah* when his wife gives birth as a result of A.I.D. Nor is there a religious imperative which would require the wife to become pregnant by artificial means since Jewish law does not consider women to be *bound* by the commandment to "be fruitful and multiply." Thus the only significant considerations prompting use of artificial insemination are those of personal desire and preference.

The crucial question, then, is whether or not artificial insemination constitutes an act of adultery. While both the donor and the physician may be guilty of an odious offense, it is only the woman who may conceivably be deemed guilty of adultery. The questions of the legitimacy of the child and the permissibility of continued conjugal relations go hand in hand with the question of adultery. If the act of insemination is not adjudged to be an act of adultery there is no reason for the child to be considered illegitimate; if the act *is* an act of adultery, it follows that the child must be considered a bastard. However, even if insemination is not equated with adultery and the child is not considered to be illegitimate, the act may be forbidden for other reasons.

Bearing these distinctions in mind it is readily recognized that the discussion which appears in the Talmud, *Chagigah* 14b, offers little illumination with regard to the permissibility of this procedure. A query was addressed to Ben Zoma with regard to whether or not a High Priest may marry a pregnant virgin. That discussion clearly indicates that at least the theoretical possibility of conception *sine concubito* was recognized by the Sages of the Talmud. However, the question under consideration was not the permissibility of the procedure itself, but the status of the mother *post-factum*.

The possibility of conception without actual intercourse is also evident in one midrashic version of the birth of Ben Sira, whose maxims are recorded in the Apocrypha. According to this source, Ben Sira was the son of the daughter of Jeremiah. The father was Jeremiah himself. Jeremiah did not commit incest but was compelled to emit semen into the waters of a bath. His daughter subsequently visited the same bathhouse and became pregnant.

Contemporary rabbinic authorities diverge with regard to whether or not A.I.D. constitutes an act of adultery. Many argue that adultery, by virtue of its very nature, requires a sexual act. In the absence of actual sexual contact with another man, the wife is not forbidden to continue to engage in marital relations with her husband and the child born of such insemination is not illegitimate.[1] Others disagree and view the receiving of another man's semen in the genital tract as an adulterous act.[2] The prohibition against adultery contained in Leviticus 18:20 reads literally, "and to the wife of your fellow you shall not give your intercourse for seed to defile her." Such phraseology is not employed in the admonitions concerning the various incestuous relations. Hence, they argue, violation of the prohibition against incest is predicated upon a sexual act while adultery is not. Those authorities who do not regard A.I.D. as adultery nevertheless view it as a repugnant violation of the marital relationship which entitles the husband to divorce his wife without being obliged to satisfy the financial obligation specified in the marriage contract.

Even those authorities who do not consider the act of insemination to be an act of adultery find that the circumstances which are usually attendant upon artificial insemination are grounds for banning A.I.D. Accepted medical procedure requires that the identity of the donor not be disclosed. Concealment of paternal identity is unconscionable according to Jewish law. Halakhah requires a three-month waiting period following divorce or the death of a husband before remarriage is permitted. The Talmud, *Yevamot* 42a, predicates this requirement upon the biblical verse "to be a God unto you and unto your seed after you" (Genesis 17:7). Rashi explains that the divine presence rests only upon those whose genealogy is clearly known. Moreover, the Talmud declares, there is concern lest the child marry a paternal sibling or that, by virtue of mistaken paternity, complications may arise with regard to levirate marriage and *chalitzah* (the ceremony of "removing the shoe" which abrogates the obligation with regard to levirate marriage). The Talmud also forbids a man to have wives in different cities for precisely the same reasons. Such a practice leads to the possibility that natural brothers and sisters, unaware of their blood relationship, may marry one another and "the land become full of immorality" (Leviticus 19:29).

This consideration has halakhic ramifications with regard to adoption procedures as well. Fear of a possible incestuous marriage mandates that an adopted child be made aware of the facts concerning his parentage. Moreover, either the child himself or a person readily accessible to him must know the identity of his natural parents. Only in this manner will the adopted child be able to determine that a prospective marriage partner is not, in fact, a forbidden relative.

A.I.H. (artificial insemination utilizing the husband's semen) poses no problem whatsoever, insofar as the act of insemination is concerned. The main question surrounds the means of obtaining the husband's semen.[3] The preferred method is retrieval of the semen from the vagina following intercourse. When failure to conceive is attributed to moderate infertility on the part of the male due to a low semen count, the problem may, at times, be corrected by combining the sperm obtained in several ejaculations.

Nevertheless, many authorities frown on this practice for a variety of reasons. One consideration auguring against A.I.H. in cases of moderate male infertility is the possibility that, in order to achieve success, the physician may be tempted to add foreign semen to that of the husband in order to enhance the chances of pregnancy. This is tantamount to A.I.D. and, hence, forbidden. Certainly, when A.I.H. is sanctioned, proper safeguards must be sought in order to assure that the semen of the husband will be used exclusively.

As noted earlier, the major difficulty concerns the means used in obtaining the husband's semen. Similar questions are encountered in procuring semen for purposes of testing and diagnosis of infertility problems. Ordinarily, ejaculation other than in the context of normal intercourse constitutes a transgression. Some authorities maintain that ejaculation for purposes of semen testing or A.I.H. does not constitute an act of "destruction" because the ultimate purpose is insemination and subsequent pregnancy. Some of these authorities nevertheless forbid actual masturbation but sanction coitus interruptus or the withdrawal method as the preferred means of semen procurement or, less preferably, the use of a condom during intercourse. Others refuse to sanction any otherwise forbidden form of ejaculation but permit the extraction of semen directly from the testicle. In light of the many conflicting views, the optimum method of semen procurement is retrieval of the semen from the vagina following intercourse. Of course, competent rabbinic advice should be sought in each individual case.

NOTES

1. See Rabbi Shalom Mordecai Schwadron, *Teshuvot Maharsham,* III, no. 268; Rabbi Aaron Walkin, *Teshuvot Zekan Aharon,* II, no. 97; Rabbi Yehoshua Baumol, *Teshuvot Emek Halakhah,* no. 68; Rabbi Ben Zion Uziel, *Mishpetei Uziel, Even ha-Ezer,* I, no. 19; Rabbi Moshe Feinstein, *Iggrot Mosheh, Even ha-Ezer,* I, no. 10; and R. Eliyahu Meir Bloch, *Ha-Pardes,* Sivan 5713.

2. Rabbi Yehudah Leib Zirelson, *Teshuvot Ma'arekhei Lev,* no. 73, and Rabbi Ovadiah Hadaya, *No'am,* I (5718), pp. 130–137. See also Rabbi Eliezer Waldenberg, *Tzitz Eli'ezer,* IX, no. 51, sec. 4.

3. The most significant discussions of this question are those of Rabbi Shalom Mordecai Schwadron, *Teshuvot Maharsham,* III, no. 268; Rabbi Aaron Walkin, *Teshuvot Zekan Aharon,* II, no. 97; Rabbi Malkiel Zvi Tenenbaum, *Teshuvot Divrei Malkiel,* IV, nos. 107–108; Rabbi Ben Zion Uziel, *Mishpetei Uziel, Even ha-Ezer,* I, no. 19; Rabbi Yehoshua Baumol, *Teshuvot Emek Halakhah,* no. 68; Rabbi Ovadiah Hadaya, *No'am* I (5718), pp. 130–137; Rabbi Ya'akov Breisch, *Teshuvot Chelkat Ya'akov,* I, no. 24; Rabbi Yitzchak Weisz, *Teshuvot Minchat Yitzchak,* IV, no. 5; Rabbi Eliezer Waldenberg, *Tzitz Eli'ezer,* IX, no. 51, secs. 4–6; Rabbi Shlomoh Zalman Auerbach, *No'am* I (5718), pp. 145–166; Rabbi Ovadiah Yosef, *Teshuvot Yabi'a Omer,* II, no. 1; and Rabbi Moshe Feinstein, *Iggrot Mosheh, Even ha-Ezer,* I, nos. 70 and 71; II, nos. 16 and 18; and III, no. 13.

15

Test-Tube Babies

With the birth of Louise Brown in the obscure mill town of Oldham in England's northwest region, science fiction of yesteryear became the reality of today. The legend of Faust and Homunculus, the little manlike creature created in a vial, has now become reality through successful development of *in vitro* fertilization.

Under normal circumstances pregnancy occurs when an ovum, an egg cell which has been released by the ovary during ovulation, is fertilized by the sperm of the male as it passes through the fallopian tube. Conception takes place when the ovum is penetrated by a single sperm from among the literally millions of sperm contained in the ejaculate deposited in the vagina. This occurs only when the sperm, after having successfully traversed the uterus, finds its way into the fallopian tube and succeeds in making contact with the ovum. Thereupon, the fertilized egg undergoes a number of cell divisions and subsequently descends into the uterus, where it becomes implanted in the uterine wall.

A significant percentage of infertility problems are the result of a disorder of the fallopian tubes. When the fallopian tubes are blocked or missing it is impossible for the sperm and ovum to make contact. The newly developed technique enables conception to occur outside the fallopian tubes. The procedure involves surgically removing the mature ovum from the ovary, placing it in a petri dish in an appropriate culture medium and adding the male sperm to the solution. The fertilized ovum is allowed to incubate in order to undergo the cell divisions which in normal pregnancy occur in the fallopian tube, and is then introduced into the uterus through the cervical os by means of a pipette. The fetus continues to develop in the uterus in an apparently normal manner. The identical technique may also be utilized to overcome moderate male infertility due to a low sperm count. A single ejaculate of a fertile male contains as many as 100 or 150 million sperm. Even though conception results from the meeting of the ovum and a single sperm, vast numbers of sperm are destroyed or rendered impotent in the process of traversing the female genital tract. Hence, males whose ejaculate contains a significantly diminished number of sperm experience difficulty in fathering children. *In vitro* fertilization would overcome this difficulty. Since the sperm are placed directly in a petri dish together with the ovum, fertilization is likely to occur even in the presence of only a small number of sperm.

As might have been anticipated, perfection of *in vitro* fertilization has given rise to a host of moral, theological, and halakhic questions. Addressing the annual *Torah she-be'al Peh* convocation in Israel, the Sephardic Chief Rabbi, Rabbi Ovadiah Yosef, gave his qualified approval to this procedure (*JTA Daily News Bulletin,* August 16, 1978). The Ashkenazic Chief Rabbi, Rabbi Shlomo Goren, is reported to view conception by such means as morally repugnant, although halakhically unobjectionable (*JTA Daily News Bulletin,* July 28, 1978; *Be-Olam ha-Rabbanut,* no. 1, Av 5738, p. 1). We shall here endeavor to delineate the specific questions. involved and to show how those questions may be resolved in light of earlier precedents in Jewish law.

In vitro fertilization has been condemned by some Catholic theologians on the grounds that such interference is not morally acceptable because it is a violation of natural law. This is precisely the same consideration which forms the basis of the Church's opposition to contraception and artificial insemination. This argument is, however, alien to Judaism. Since Judaism does not posit a doctrine of natural law as such, these practices, according to Jewish teaching, must be examined solely in light of possible infraction of biblical proscriptions. In the absence of a specific prohibition, man is free to utilize scientific knowledge in order to overcome impediments of nature.

The first question which must be examined is the moral legitimacy of research involving fetal experimentation. The birth of a test-tube baby could not, at the time, have taken place in the United States. All such research was abruptly terminated in 1975, when the Department of Health, Education and Welfare was barred from funding *in vitro* fertilization experiments in the absence of prior approval of a national ethics advisory board. Such a board was not constituted until January 1978. The Department of Health, Education and Welfare has only recently approved experimentation of this nature. The crucial issue is that of increased risk of chromosomal abnormalities leading to physical and mental defects when the ovum is fertilized outside the body. It is entirely possible that some aspect of the experimental technique may cause genetic damage. Moreover, it is estimated that as many as a half of all pregnancies are spontaneously terminated by the time of implantation. The mechanism responsible for this phenomenon is not fully known, but there is reason to believe that in many instances this is nature's method of providentially preventing the development of a deformed fetus. Artificial maintenance of the zygote outside the body during this early stage of gestation may prevent the natural elimination of a deformed fetus.

The ethical implications of experimentation which may result in the birth of a defective fetus have been analyzed by a leading bioethicist, Professor Paul Ramsey of Princeton University.[1] Professor Ramsey argues that *in vitro* fertilization followed by implantation is an immoral experiment upon a possible future life since no researcher can exclude the possibility that he will do irreparable damage to the child-to-be: "We ought not to choose for another the hazards he must bear, while choosing at the same time to give him life in which to bear them and to suffer our chosen experimentations."

This argument, insofar as it applies to artificial conception, is entirely consistent with the norms of Torah ethics. Jewish law does not sanction abortion motivated solely by a desire to eliminate a defective fetus, nor does it sanction sterile marriage as a means of preventing transmission of hereditary disorders. However, it does discourage marriages which would lead to the conception of such children. The Gemara, *Yevamot* 64b, declares that a man should not marry into an epileptic or leprous family, i.e., a family in which three members have suffered from these diseases. This ruling is obviously a eugenic measure designed to prevent the birth of defective children. It follows, *a fortiori,* that overt intervention in natural processes which might cause defects in the fetus would be viewed with opprobrium by Judaism.

Despite the happy initial success in the case of the Brown infant, it will require the birth and maturation through adolescence and into adulthood of a significant number of healthy and normal test-tube babies before the technique may be viewed as morally acceptable. When, and if, it has in fact been demonstrated that the procedure poses no risk to the fetus there can be no objection to the utilization of this technique on the basis of the fact that the original experimentation was morally unconscionable. As observed by Dr. Daniel Callahan, "The history of medicine is full of instances where things were done unethically but led to benefits for people."[2] An obvious example, from the perspective of Jewish law, is that of post-mortem examinations which were halakhically unwarranted at the time of their performance but which have led to acquisition of potentially life-saving information. Jewish ethics knows of no *Miranda* principle which would bar the use after the fact of information obtained by illicit means.

It should also be stressed that, even in the absence of moral or halakhic objections, no woman is required to submit to *in vitro* fertilization. The obligations of women, whether by reason of the scriptural exhortation to populate the universe, "He created it not a waste, He formed it to be inhabited" (Isaiah 45:18), or by virtue of marital contract, are limited to bearing children by means of natural intercourse. In a different context, Rabbi Moshe Feinstein, *Iggrot Mosheh, Even ha-Ezer,* III, no. 12, expresses the view that a woman, while bound to assume the pain usually associated with normal childbirth, is under no obligation to conceive when faced with the likelihood of unusual and extraordinary pain. Furthermore, it appears to this writer that the comments of *Tosafot, Yevamot* 70a and *Pesachim* 28b, establish the principle that one need not assume the pain and risk of a surgical procedure for purposes of fulfilling even an obligatory *mitzvah.*[3] The husband's obligations with regard to procreation under such circumstances are discussed by the

Shulchan Arukh, Even ha-Ezer 154:10–11, and commentaries thereon.

The means employed in procuring sperm for purposes of *in vitro* fertilization do, however, pose a halakhic problem. Jewish law forbids ejaculation other than within the context of intercourse as *hotza'at zera le-vatalah*—destruction of the seed. The question is whether or not semen procurement designed to promote procreation is deemed to be *le-vatalah*. The identical question has been raised in the past, both with regard to semen testing in cases of suspected male infertility and in connection with artificial insemination utilizing the semen of the husband. As has been noted earlier, this question is analyzed in detail by many halakhic authorities.[4]

Removal of semen from the vaginal tract following normal coitus for *in vitro* fertilization would appear to be regarded by most authorities as the optimal method. Although some authorities forbid emission of semen for subsequent insemination other than in the course of coitus, others sanction this practice but disagree with regard to the means of procurement. Some authorities advise that semen be obtained by means of coitus interruptus. Others sanction the use of a condom as well. The permissibility of masturbation for this purpose is a matter of dispute. Such procedures can, of course, be sanctioned only if the sperm of the husband is used exclusively. Under no circumstances should the sperm of any person other than the husband be utilized. Proper safeguards must be established in order to assure that this should not occur even unwittingly.

There are of course a host of other questions which present themselves: Does the husband fulfill his obligation with regard to procreation by means of *in vitro* fertilization? Does a filial relationship exist between the father and a child born in this manner? Does the child enjoy the status of the father as a Kohen or Levite? Is the child considered to be an heir to his father's estate? These questions have been analyzed with regard to children born of artificial insemination and such discussions appear to be equally germane to the case of children born as a result of *in vitro* fertilization. In any event, the resolution of these questions has no bearing upon the permissibility of *in vitro* fertilization.

It should be noted that one aspect of the *in vitro*

procedure—as reportedly performed—does present particular cause for concern. The human female is endowed at birth with as many as a million or more ova. These egg cells mature, ripen, and are normally released between puberty and menopause at the rate of approximately one a month. It is reported that, in order to enhance the chances of success of *in vitro* fertilization without resorting to repeated surgical removal of mature ova, hormones are administered in order to hasten maturation of the egg cells, so that multiple ova may be removed at one time. All ova removed in this manner are exposed to the male sperm. This permits the fertilization of more than a single ovum. The fertilized ova are then examined and carefully monitored for any sign of chromosomal abnormality. Finally, a single blastocyst is selected for implantation and the remainder are destroyed.

The procedure, when carried out in this manner, poses the question of the permissibility of destroying a developing embryo. Many halakhic authorities have ruled that the prohibition against feticide is operative immediately following conception, while others maintain that no prohibition exists within the first forty days of gestation. In the case of *in vitro* fertilization the entire question may, of course, readily be sidestepped by limiting the procedure to the fertilization of a single ovum.[5]

Development and perfection of *in vitro* techniques may, in time, make it possible to select not only the sex but also other genetic characteristics, such as the color of the baby's eyes, IQ, adult height, etc. Indeed, given the almost infinite number of ova and sperm available and the rapid advances now being made in the field of genetics, it is not at all inconceivable that genetic characteristics may be ordered to conform with virtually any parental preference or whim. The moral, genetic, and societal implications of such practices are truly awesome. Nevertheless, the distinction between capricious genetic manipulation and *in vitro* fertilization which stimulates natural procreation and is designed solely to alleviate infertility due to abnormality of the fallopian tubes should be readily apparent.

If properly safeguarded, *in vitro* fertilization may, in time, prove to be a highly beneficial development. Certainly, indiscriminate tampering with nature is dangerous and immoral. Utmost vigilance must be maintained lest we fashion a

Huxley-type world in which eugenic selection becomes the norm. Yet, if properly controlled and not permitted to become a substitute for normal human procreation, this revolutionary technique can be a welcome means of bestowing the happiness and fulfillment of parenthood upon otherwise childless couples.

NOTES

1. "Shall We 'Reproduce'?" *Journal of the American Medical Association,* vol. 220, no. 10 (June 5, 1972), pp. 1346–1350, and vol. 220, no. 11 (June 12, 1972), pp. 1480–1485; and *The Ethics of Fetal Research* (Yale University Press, 1975).
2. *New York Times,* July 27, 1978, p. A 16, col. 3.
3. Cf., however, Rashba and Me'iri, *Yevamot* 71b.
4. See above, chapter 14, note 1.
5. It has recently been reported that superovulation in order to make possible the removal of multiple ova has been abandoned because, for reasons which are not completely understood, implantation proved to be unsuccessful. Apparently, the hormone administered to stimulate maturation of multiple ova in some manner interferes with the ability of the uterus to accept the fertilized ovum. All successful implantations have involved the fertilization of a single ovum obtained through natural maturation. Dr. Mason Andrews, chairman of the department of obstetrics and gynecology of the Eastern Virginia Medical School, which operates the In Vitro Fertilization Clinic in Norfolk, Virginia, is quoted as saying that no attempt is made to test for chromosomal abnormality. Implantation later than the eight- or sixteen-cell stage has proved to be unsuccessful. Microbiopsy for purposes of chromosomal study of the embryo, a technique developed by Dr. Pierre Soupart of Vanderbilt University, is performed at the 128-cell stage at which point the embryo has developed an outer wall from which a few cells can be removed without harming the embryo. Regrettably, detailed descriptions of the techniques employed in *in vitro* fertilization have not appeared in scientific journals. See, however, Anne Taylor Fleming, "New Frontiers in Conception," *The New York Times Magazine,* July 20, 1980. Presumably, this information will be included by Robert Edwards and Patrick Steptoe in their forthcoming book, *A Matter of Life* to be published by William Morrow, New York, 1980.

16

Host-Mothers

Any parent who has at one time or another been exposed by his children to the captivating Dr. Seuss fantasy, *Horton Hatches the Egg,* will recall the dilemma around which that tale centers: to whom does the offspring rightfully belong, to the irresponsible mother who abandoned it or to the faithful elephant who guarded and protected the egg over a span of months? The fictional solution may be both too facile—and too equitable—for real life. Preposterous and far-fetched as the situation may appear to be, the problems it poses may be upon us before long. We find ourselves in an age in which the science fiction of yesterday is rapidly becoming the reality of today; the hypothetical curiosity of today may well become the commonplace of tomorrow. These unfolding realia often carry in their wake hitherto unexamined moral and religious questions. Perhaps in no area is this more evident than in the field of embryology. Recent experimental developments indicate that it may soon become possible to remove a naturally fertilized ovum from the womb of a pregnant mother and to reimplant it in the uterus of another woman. The embryo would then remain in the womb of the "host-mother" throughout the period of gestation until birth.

Rabbi Immanuel Jakobovits, Chief Rabbi of Great Britain, aptly characterizes such practices as offensive to moral sensitivities when resorted to as a convenience in order to avoid the encumbrances of pregnancy. Certainly all will agree that "to use another person as an 'incubator' and then take from her the child she carried and delivered for a fee is a revolting degradation of maternity and an affront to human dignity."

Convenience is, however, not the only conceivable motive which may prompt a procedure of this nature. Medical factors may well make it impossible for the natural mother to carry her baby to term. Would Halakhah sanction the use of a "host-mother" for the purpose of saving the fetus? If such a procedure is performed, with or without halakhic sanction, who is regarded as the mother in the eyes of Halakhah: the natural mother or the host-mother?

As yet, very little has been written on this subject, although a related question has received some attention in rabbinic literature.[1] Maternal identity became an issue in a case in which the ovary of a fertile woman was transplanted into the body of a previously barren woman in an attempt to enable her to become pregnant and bear children. Which of the two women is to be considered the mother of the child in the eyes of Jewish law? Cases involving a donor who is a married woman pose yet another question. Is the husband of the woman receiving the ovarian transplant thereafter permitted to engage in intercourse with his wife? Is the husband who has sexual relations with a wife carrying a transplanted reproductive organ of another married woman guilty of adultery? The latter question can be dismissed since the source of specific organs has no bearing upon the halakhic definition of adultery.

Furthermore, a transplanted organ is deemed to have become an integral part of the body of the recipient. For this reason, the recipient of an ovarian transplant must also be considered the mother of any child subsequently conceived. Since it is the mother who nurtures and sustains the embryo, it is the female parent alone who determines the species of the offspring. Accordingly, it is the identity of the mother which is transferred to members of an interspecies. Thus progeny born of interbreeding are members of the same species as the mother. There is, however, a conflicting talmudic opinion which asserts that "the father's seed is to be considered" (*Chullin* 79a). Even proponents of this latter view will concede that with regard to ovarian transplants the identity of the donor need not be considered in establishing maternity. "The father's seed is to be considered" because the father plays a dynamic role in the birth of the offspring. The ovary alone is an inert organ and incapable of reproduction were it not for the physiological contributions of the recipient.

To a significant degree, the identical argumentation may be applied in determining the maternity of a child born of a fertilized ovum implanted in the womb of a host-mother. It is the host-mother who nurtures the embryo and sustains gestation. However, the role of the natural mother in determination of identity is a dynamic one and analogous to that of "the seed of the father." It may therefore be argued that, according to those who assert with reference to classification of hybrids that "the seed of the father is to be considered," in the case of an already fertilized ovum, the maternal relationship between the child and the donor mother is to be "considered" no less than "the seed of the father." Consideration must also be given to the possibility that perhaps two maternal relationships may exist simultaneously just as maternal and paternal relationships exist at one and the same time. The child would then, in effect, have two "mothers," the donor mother and the host-mother.

According to some authorities, however, the donor mother alone may be viewed as the mother in the eyes of Jewish law. There are those who maintain that the prohibition against feticide is applicable from the moment of conception and deem the fetus to be a nascent human being even in the earliest stages of gestation. According to this view, the zygote may perhaps be viewed as having already acquired identity and parentage.

The discussion thus far applies only to the transplantation of a fertilized ovum removed shortly after conception. Transplantation of an embryo in later stages of development presents a rather different question. What has preceded is based upon fragmentary sources and is but one aspect of a topic whose many ramifications have yet to be examined.[2] There is indeed a great need for such examination and analysis for the transformations which may soon be wrought by scientific advances in this field touch upon the very foundations of the sanctity of the family.

NOTES

1. R. Yekutiel Aryeh Kamelhar, *Ha-Talmud u-Mada'ei ha-Tevel,* pp. 44–45.

2. See the recently published article by R. Moshe Hirschler, in his *Halakhah u-Refu'ah* (Jerusalem, 5740), pp. 307–320.

17

Abortion

Judaism regards the killing of an unborn child to be a serious moral offense. An abortion may be performed only for the gravest of reasons, and even then, only subsequent to consultation with a competent rabbinic authority.

In some circles confusion has arisen with regard to the status of the fetus by virtue of the fact that feticide on the part of a Jew is not considered to be a capital crime. It must be stressed that the lessened severity of the statutory punishment imposed upon the malefactor in no way mitigates the odious nature of the act.

It is clear, on the basis of the Mishnah, *Oholot* 7:6, that the life of the mother takes precedence over that of the unborn child. Thus, when "hard travail" of labor endangers the life of the mother an embryotomy may be performed in order to save her life. The Mishnah, while certainly acknowledging that the fetus is endowed with a "right to life," establishes the principle that the fetus' title to life is subordinate to that of the mother, and hence the life of the unborn fetus may be sacrificed in order to preserve that of the mother. However, Maimonides, in codifying this law (*Hilkhot Rotzeach* 1:9) is not content to state simply that the life of the fetus is subordinate to that of the mother but adds a further explanation. He describes the child as being, in effect, an aggressor engaged in "pursuing" the life of the mother. Maimonides' incorporation of this rationale in his Code has given rise to considerable discussion and analysis and is the primary source of the view of numerous authorities who maintain that Jewish law forbids even therapeutic abortion in non life-threatening situations. By invoking the "law of pursuit" Maimonides indicates that the life of the fetus is forfeit only because it is, in some sense, an aggressor. When the fetus is not the proximate cause of the threat to the mother this rationale does not apply. Maimonides' comment also serves to establish that feticide is a form of (non-capital) homicide. It is this source which led the Chief Rabbinate of Israel, in the course of public debate over abortion legislation, to declare the performance of an abortion to be an act of murder.[1]

Other authorities maintain that the ban against feticide is subsumed under other prohibited activities, such as illicit "wounding" or "destruction of the seed." According to those authorities, the performance of an abortion may be warranted for purposes of preserving maternal health as well as maternal life.

No authority permits an abortion which is non-therapeutic in nature. There are early rabbinic authorities who expressly declare that ritual laws such as *Shabbat* observance and fasting on *Yom Kippur* are suspended in order to preserve the life of the fetus. Suspension of such significant religious observances is clearly incompatible with indiscriminate license to destroy fetal life.

Both the argument that a prospective mother may seek an abortion for any reason because denial of this right would interfere with her "right to privacy" as well as the argument that a decision to abort is entirely a matter between a woman and her physician must be rejected as incompatible with Jewish teaching. As has been shown earlier, Judaism teaches that man does not enjoy unrestricted proprietary rights with regard to his own body, much less so with regard to the body of an unborn child. Furthermore, the fetus is not merely an appendage to the mother, but is a being in its own right. The Gemara concludes that the embryo is endowed with a soul at the moment of conception.[2] Moreover, the Sages taught, "There are three partners in [the generation of] man: the father, the mother, and God."[3] Accordingly, a decision to terminate pregnancy is not one which is within the exclusive domain of the mother.

The question of the inviolate nature of fetal life during the first forty days following conception is a matter of some dispute. The Gemara, *Yevamot* 69b, states that the daughter of a priest who became widowed shortly after marriage to an Israelite may partake of *terumah* until forty days have elapsed following the consummation of her marriage, despite the fact that she has become a widow in the interim. Permission to eat *terumah* is a privilege accorded an unmarried daughter of a priest or a widowed daughter who has no children. Thus, the widowed daughter is not barred from partaking of *terumah* if she is not pregnant. Even if pregnant, she may eat *terumah,* states the Gemara, during the first forty days of gestation because the embryo is considered to be "mere water" during this period. Some authorities cite this ruling as an indication that fetal development during the first forty days of gestation is insufficient to warrant independent standing in the eyes of Jewish law. Others maintain that although the embryo is as yet undeveloped, and by virtue of its undeveloped state cannot prevent its mother from partaking of *terumah* during this period, nevertheless, its potential for development into a viable human being is, in itself, sufficient to guarantee it an inviolable claim to life.

It is well established that the quality of life to be anticipated if the fetus is carried to term is not, in itself, a sufficient reason for the performance of an abortion. The status of abnormal and malformed human beings is well defined in Halakhah. Physical or mental abnormalities do not affect the human status of the individual or his right to life. The thirteenth-century authority, Rabbi Judah the Pious, issued a definitive ruling forbidding the termination of the life of a monsterlike child born with the teeth and tail of an animal.[4] Indeed, the interlocutor raised the question only because of fear aroused by reports that the creature would later "eat people." A later authority ruled unequivocally that the killing of even a grotesquely malformed child possessing animal features constitutes an act of murder.[5] The issue of a human mother, no matter how deformed, enjoys human status and may not be destroyed either by overt act or by passively allowing it to die of starvation.

These considerations apply with equal weight to the destruction of an abnormal or deformed fetus. Accordingly, the consensus of contemporary authorities is that pregnancy may not be terminated even if it is known that the baby has suffered damage as a result of rubella contracted by the mother through ingestion of thalidomide or as the result of a congenital defect.[6] Those authorities who adopt an opposing view and permit an abortion during the early stages of pregnancy do so, not on the basis of the deformity *per se,* but in consideration of the physical and psychic difficulties the rearing of such a child will place upon the mother.[7] In light of the multi-faceted factors which must be assessed in reaching a halakhic determination, rabbinic advice should be sought on a case-by-case basis.

For similar reasons most authorities rule that termination of a pregnancy resulting from rape is not permissible. However, immediate post-coital contraceptive measures undertaken prior to fertilization of the ovum present a different but complex halakhic question. Immediate removal of the semen by means of a suction device operated by a female (who is, according to many authorities, not bound by the prohibition against "destroying the seed") would be warranted, at least according to some authorities, particularly if the rapist is a non-Jew.[8] Again, rabbinic advice should be sought on a case-by-case basis.

Destruction of a fetus by a non-Jew is a matter of even greater severity. Jewish law recognizes two distinct, divinely revealed codes of law. One is binding upon Jews as a result of the Sinaitic covenant; the second, which is more limited in scope, is known as the Seven Commandments of the Sons of Noah. This latter code is binding upon all non-Jews. Judaism teaches that Noachides are specifically enjoined from destroying fetal life upon penalty of death. Consequently, any aid extended to a gentile in the performance of an abortion is a violation of the precept, "Thou shalt not place a stumbling-block before the blind" (Leviticus 19:14).

It is instructive to note that, historically speaking, societies which condoned abortion invariably practiced infanticide as well. Prior to the advent of Judaism, the ancient societies of the West practiced abortion to a greater or lesser degree. By the same token, "With the exception of the Jews, infanticide has from time immemorial been the accepted procedure for disposing not only of deformed or sickly infants, but of all such newborns as might strain the resources of the individual family or the larger community."[9] Nor has infanticide been unknown in modern times. As recently as 1862, a certain Dr. William Ryan wrote in the conclusion of a work entitled *Infanticide: Its*

Law, Prevention and History: "We cannot ignore the fact that the crime of infanticide, as well as that of criminal abortion, is widespread and on the increase."

From the historical perspective, it is not at all surprising that in the aftermath of the 1970 Supreme Court decision in *Roe v. Wade* legalizing abortion, attempts are being made to effect what is tantamount to the legalization of infanticide. The prominent situation ethicist Professor Joseph Fletcher has argued that if the life of a mongoloid baby can be "ended prenatally, why should it not be ended neonatally (i.e. just after birth)?"[10] Dr. James Watson, co-discoverer of the DNA double-helix, offers a novel and subtle approach. Contemporary society regards feticide as morally acceptable, but infanticide as morally repugnant. Why not redefine birth? In effect, Watson argues that all that is needed is a rejection of the traditional notion which equates birth with parturition and the substitution of a new definition. In an article which appeared in the AMA's socio-economic magazine, *Prism,* he writes, " . . . if a child were not declared alive until three days after birth, then all parents could be allowed the choice that only a few are given under the present system." In other words, the parents would be offered a second chance for an abortion. In a similar vein, England's Nobel Prize–winning biologist, Dr. Francis Crick, has advocated legislation under which newborn babies would not be considered legally alive until they are two days old and certified as healthy by medical examiners. Michael Tooley, professor of philosophy at Stanford University, would grant even greater latitude. He argues that human babies even after birth are no more than kittens and cannot be bearers of rights until they have self-consciousness of themselves as persons. Accordingly, he finds no reason to view with disapprobation the killing of any child within the first two weeks of life.[11]

Judaism, of course, opposes abortion on intrinsic grounds, and not simply because it may lead to infanticide. The erosion of sensitivity to the sanctity of human life does, however, magnify the odium associated with abortion.

The net effect of the ban against feticide, on whatever grounds it is based, is to endow the unborn fetus with a "right to life." Whether the unborn child is a "person in the full sense" or simply a "fetus" is irrelevant insofar as the fetus' title to life is concerned. It is only when respect for the fetal right to life poses a threat to the mother that a question arises.

Although the physiological facts are not germane in determining the permissibility of non-therapeutic abortion, it is instructive to note that on purely medical grounds it is difficult to sustain the argument that the fetus is not a human being. Essential criteria of life can be ascertained in the womb even in early stages of pregnancy. The presence of heart function and brain activity have been noted in embryos at six to eight weeks. The most recent investigations disclose that a formed cortex can be perceived visually in the fetal brain on the fortieth day of gestation and that brain waves can be discerned by means of an EEG by the forty-third day. According to the criteria for the establishment of time of death proposed by the Harvard Ad Hoc Committee (which, incidentally, as will be shown in a later chapter, are rejected by Halakhah as being too limited in their concept of life), one may conclude that death has occurred only if the patient is unresponsive to external stimuli, if reflexes are absent, if there are no spontaneous movements or respiratory efforts, and if an EEG reveals the absence of brain activity. If any of these criteria are manifest, life must be present. Paul Ramsey and others have argued quite cogently that since the fetus does respond to pain, does make respiratory efforts, does move spontaneously, and does manifest electroencephalographic activity, it must be deemed a human life even on the basis of the very liberal views of the Harvard Committee.[12]

It should be clearly understood that the question of whether or not a fetus is a "person" or a "full human being" is largely irrelevant in a halakhic context. Judaism regards all forms of human life as sacred, from the formation of germ plasm in the cell of the sperm until decomposition of the body after death. To be sure, applicable *halakhot* vary in an appropriate manner from stage to stage along this continuum. It is the nature of the prohibition and the specific regulations which are significant, not matters of nomenclature which are of no halakhic significance.

NOTES

1. *JTA Daily News Bulletin,* Dec. 7, 1974.
2. *Sanhedrin* 91b.
3. *Kiddushin* 30b.
4. *Sefer Chasidim,* no. 196.
5. R. Eliezer Fleckeles, *Teshuvah me-Ahavah,* I, no. 53.
6. Rabbi Moshe Yonah Zweig, *No'am* III, 36–56; Rabbi I. Y. Unterman, *No'am* VI, 1–11; and Rabbi Moshe Feinstein, *Ha-Pardes,* Nisan 5738.
7. Rabbi Eliezer Waldenberg, *Tzitz Eli'ezer* IX, no. 51, chap. 3, and *Assia,* Adar 5736.
8. R. Eliezer Chaim Deutsch, *Pri ha-Sadeh* IV, no. 50; R. Yeruchem Yehudah Perilman, *Or Gadol,* no. 31.
9. William L. Langer, "Infanticide: A Historical Survey," *History of Childhood,* Winter 1974, pp. 353–354. See also the comments of Professor Paul Ramsey, "Protecting the Unborn," *Commonweal,* May 31, 1974, p. 310.
10. *Atlantic Monthly,* April 1962.
11. "Abortion and Infanticide," *Philosophy and Public Affairs,* Fall 1972.
12. To this may be added the poignant observation that, even in the post–*Roe v. Wade* era, a stillbirth is recorded simultaneously as a birth and a death. By law, a birth certificate as well as a death certificate must be filed, indicating that, at least for purposes of registration, human life does exist prior to birth.

18

Genetic Screening

There exist a host of diseases and congenital abnormalities which are the result of genetic causes. Medical science has discovered ways of identifying persons who may potentially become parents of offspring affected in this way. It is also possible to determine during the course of pregnancy whether or not a fetus is afflicted with certain abnormalities by means of a test known as amniocentesis.

The genetic disorder most common among Jews is Tay-Sachs disease. Tay-Sachs disease is a fatal, inherited condition. A child afflicted with this disorder appears normal at birth and may develop normally until five or six months of age. At that point normal development of the nervous system ceases. Over the next few months the infant gradually loses the ability to sit and in time becomes unable to hold up his head. As physical deterioration progresses, the child becomes blind, becomes subject to frequent convulsive seizures, loses the ability to swallow food and its limbs become stiff. Death usually occurs in the third or fourth year of life.

Tay-Sachs disease is caused by a genetic mutation. The disease appears only in a child who has inherited a pair of genes both of which are defective. One of the pair is inherited from the mother; the other from the father. The parents, each of whom is the carrier of a defective gene which may be transmitted to his or her offspring, are themselves perfectly normal both physically and mentally.

Diseases resulting from genetic mutation are often limited to specific ethnic groups. Tay-Sachs is such a disease and is prevalent among children of Ashkenazic Jews. On the other hand, phenylketonuria, a defective gene common among white gentiles, is very rare among Jews. Similarly, sickle-cell anemia is prevalent among Negroes. The carrier-rate of Tay-Sachs disease among Jews of Central and East European ancestry is believed to be about one person in thirty. Since both parents must be carriers for the child to be affected, it may be assumed that statistically one in nine hundred Jewish couples may have a Tay-Sachs child. Should two such people marry and have children, the risk that they will have an infant afflicted with Tay-Sachs disease is one in four with each pregnancy. This is so because each normal parent possesses two genes, one of which is normal, the other defective. The child inherits only one of these genes, giving him a fifty percent chance of inheriting the abnormal gene from each of his parents. If a defective gene is inherited from one parent but a normal gene from the other, the child will be normal. The statistical probability of his inheriting two defective genes, one from each parent, is 1/2 × 1/2, which equals 1/4. Since one individual in thirty is a carrier, one in 3600 babies (1/30 × 1/30 × 1/4) will be a victim of Tay-Sachs disease. In the non-Jewish population only one individual in 300 is a carrier. Hence, statistically, only one marriage in 90,000 is between two carriers, and only one baby in 360,000 is a victim of Tay-Sachs disease. A similar pattern applies with regard to other congenital disorders produced by a recessive gene.

During the past several years, medical centers in a number of cities have initiated large-scale campaigns in a massive attempt to eliminate the disease. A carrier can be identified by means of a simple blood test. The enzyme responsible for the condition normally leaks from cells into the circulating plasma. The absence of this enzyme in the plasma indicates that the individual is a carrier. The absence of the enzyme can also be detected in cells shed from the skin of the fetus into the amniotic fluid. It is thus possible to make a diagnosis of an affected fetus *in utero* by means of amniocentesis, which involves tapping the amniotic fluid in the uterus and examination of fetal cells.

Physicians now urgently recommend that rabbis refer prospective brides and grooms to a local testing center so that a blood test may be performed in order to identify carriers of

Tay-Sachs disease. As a result of the test the following recommendations are made by the medical personnel involved:

1. If the screening test for the carrier state is positive in only one member of the couple no danger exists with regard to the offspring of that marriage. Such individuals are counseled with regard to the significance of the mutation and are urged to have their own offspring tested for future reference and counseling.
2. If both members of the couple are carriers:
   a. They are warned that the risks of bearing a Tay-Sachs child are one in four with each pregnancy.
   b. They are counseled with regard to the alternatives to having their own natural children.
   c. They are admonished that should they proceed to have their own children, fetal monitoring should be undertaken. If a Tay-Sachs fetus is identified the common medical practice is to recommend an abortion.

The elimination of Tay Sachs and other genetic diseases is, of course, a goal to which all concerned individuals subscribe. However, the means by which this desideratum is to be attained must be examined carefully because of the halakhic questions involved.

Of serious concern is the advice not to have children when both prospective parents are identified as carriers of a genetic disease. This is one of the options routinely suggested by genetic counselors.

The obligation with regard to procreation is not suspended simply because of the statistical probability that some children of the union may be deformed or abnormal. While the couple may quite properly be counseled with regard to the risks of having a Tay-Sachs child, it should be stressed that failure to bear natural children is not a halakhically viable alternative.[1] As has been indicated earlier, artificial insemination using donor semen is not an acceptable solution.

Of at least equal, if not graver, concern is the proposal that fetal monitoring be performed with a view toward termination of the pregnancy if the fetus be identified as a victim of Tay-Sachs disease.

The fear that a child may be born physically malformed or mentally deficient does not in itself justify recourse to abortion. At present, amniocentesis cannot be performed prior to the fourth or fifth month of pregnancy. The consensus of opinion among contemporary rabbinic authorities is that at so late a stage in pregnancy abortion is permissible only if continuation of pregnancy constitutes a threat to the life of the mother. In situations in which amniocentesis is performed for purposes of diagnosing a condition for which a medical remedy is available, e.g., blood-group incompatibility which can be treated by exchange transfusion, the physician is not only permitted but is obligated to perform the amniocentesis, even repeatedly. However, amniocentesis carried out solely for the purpose of diagnosing severe genetic defects such as Tay-Sachs disease serves no therapeutic purpose. Since the sole available medical remedy following diagnosis of severe genetic defects is abortion of the fetus, which is not sanctioned by Halakhah in such instances,[2] amniocentesis, under these conditions, does not serve as an aid in treatment of the patient and is not halakhically permissible. Initiation of this procedure in the absence of a therapeutic goal poses a pointless medical risk to both mother and fetus and also constitutes an act of *chavalah*—an unwarranted assault upon the mother.[3]

Blood-testing programs as a screening method for the identification of carriers of Tay-Sachs disease before marriage pose no halakhic problem. In fact, one prominent contemporary authority urges such testing prior to marriage.[4] It must be emphasized, however, that when Tay-Sachs screening is carried out before marriage and both prospective bride and groom have been identified as Tay-Sachs carriers they must be counseled that Judaism does not sanction a sterile union.

Certainly, marriages which are likely to lead to the birth of defective children should not be encouraged. In what is historically perhaps the oldest recorded item of genetic counseling, the Talmud counsels that a man should not marry into a family of lepers or epileptics. Yet, once such a marriage has been contracted, the obligation to "be fruitful and multiply" is in no way mitigated. Indeed, the commandment with regard to procreation is fulfilled even if the only children born of the union are mentally or physically defective, so long as they, in turn, become parents.[5]

The Talmud emphasizes that fear of undesirable traits in progeny, even when such fears are firmly grounded, does not constitute legitimate grounds for abstention from procreation. The Talmud relates that it was revealed to King Hezekiah by means of the "holy spirit" that his children would be morally deficient. He therefore chose not to marry. The prophet Isaiah was sent to him with the message, "Thus said the Lord, set your house in order, for you shall die and not live." The Talmud interprets this verse as meaning, "You shall die in this world and not live in the World-to-Come," indicating that this severe punishment was to be meted out because Hezekiah made no attempt to sire children. In response to Hezekiah's protestation that he was prompted to refrain from becoming a father because of his realization that his children would not be virtuous, Isaiah retorts, "What have you to do with the secrets of the All-Merciful? That which you were commanded you should have done, and that which is pleasing to the Holy One, blessed be He, let Him do!"[6] Man is obliged to fulfill the divinely imposed obligation to "be fruitful and multiply"; all else is in the hands of God.

To this may be added an interesting historical footnote. The risk of a serious genetic defect in cases in which both parents are afflicted with congenital syphilis is very great. Should such a couple actually become parents of a child afflicted with congenital blindness and who, in addition, survives for only ten days, one could readily sympathize with their reluctance to attempt another pregnancy or even with their decision to abort the fetus should pregnancy occur. But, as one writer recently pointed out, had one such couple acted in this way, Beethoven would never have been born![7]

The emotional distress which an engaged couple are bound to experience upon discovering that they are both carriers is certainly a factor auguring for earlier identification of the carrier state. Sensitivity to the dictates of Halakhah, which precludes both abortion and a sterile union, would indicate that the most propitious time for such screening is childhood or early adolescence. Early awareness of a carrier state, particularly when determination can be made on a mass scale, would contribute greatly to alleviating the gravity of the situation.

It has been argued that genetic screening among adolescents should be discouraged because it would generate psychological stress among those identified as carriers. Whether or not such stress need be feared is a matter of some debate.[8] It is, however, incontrovertible that there is no objective basis for any such psychological trauma. The carrier state for any genetic disorder in no way compromises the health of the carrier. The carrier is a perfectly normal human being in every respect. In fact, there is some evidence that carriers are at an advantage insofar as resistance to tuberculosis is concerned, and there may also exist a correlation between the carrier state and superior intelligence. The carrier's sole concern is the choice of a marriage partner. If the carrier's spouse is not a carrier as well, there is no possibility of bearing Tay-Sachs children. If the significance of these facts is properly understood, there is no reason for trauma to occur. Public education campaigns can do much to cause this to be fully appreciated within the Jewish community.

There should certainly be no question of stigmatization of individuals identified as carriers. Carriers are themselves in no way afflicted, and there is no rational basis for a non-carrier to consider a carrier to be undesirable as a marriage partner. It cannot be overemphasized that a medical problem exists only in a marriage in which *both* partners are Tay-Sachs carriers. Since Tay-Sachs is a genetically recessive abnormality there is no possibility whatsoever that a child may suffer from hereditary Tay-Sachs disease if only one of his parents is a carrier. Children born of a union between a carrier and a non-carrier are at risk only of themselves being carriers. Since a Tay-Sachs carrier is in no way less healthy than a non-carrier such a child suffers no disadvantage save the advisability of exercising prudence in determining that his or her marriage partner is a non-carrier. Thus, there is absolutely no reason for any stigma to be associated with the carrier state.

NOTES

1. *Iggrot Mosheh, Even ha-Ezer,* no. 62. See also *Teshuvot Levushei Mordekhai,* IV, no. 68; *Teshuvot Afarkata de-Anya,* no. 169; and *Teshuvot Minchat Yitzchak,* III, no. 26, sec. 1.

2. Cf. J. David Bleich, *Contemporary Halakhic Problems* (New York, 1977), pp. 112–115. The dissenting view there examined has been emphatically rejected by R. Moshe Feinstein, *Ha-Pardes,* Nisan 5738; see J. David Bleich, "Abortion in Halakhic Literature," *Jewish Bioethics,* ed. Fred Rosner and J. David Bleich (New York, 1979), p. 161, and p. 175, note 97.

3. For the results of a recent study of the adverse effects of amniocentesis, see "An Assessment of the Hazards of Amniocentesis: Report to the Medical Research Council by Their Working Party on Amniocentesis," *British Journal of Obstetrics and Gynaecology,* vol. LXXXV (1978), Supplement, no. 2. In this study, increased fetal loss attributable to amniocentesis was found to be between 1.0 and 1.5 percent, and a similar increase in certain major types of infant morbidity was found to be between 1.0 and 1.5 percent. The total adverse effects in terms of combined fetal mortality and infant morbidity is estimated as being between 2 and 3 percent.

4. Rabbi Moshe Feinstein, unpublished letter dated 18 Adar 5733.

5. See *Teshuvot Maharil,* no. 223; also cited in *Bet Yosef, Even ha-Ezer* 1.

6. *Berakhot* 10a.

7. Maurice Baring, quoted by David Daube, *Medical and Genetic Ethics,* pamphlet published by the Oxford Centre for Postgraduate Hebrew Studies (Oxford, 1976), p. 8, note 1.

8. Possible psychological consequences of carrier identification are discussed by E. Beck, S. Blaichman, and C. R. Seriver, "Advocacy and Compliance in Genetic Screening," *New England Journal of Medicine* 291:1166–1170, 1974; M. M. Kaback, R. S. Zeiger, L. W. Reynolds, *et al.,* "Tay-Sachs Disease: A Model for the Control of Recessive Genetic Disorders," *Proceedings of the Fourth International Conference,* Vienna, Austria, Sept. 2–8, 1973, and *Excerpta Medica,* 1974, pp. 248–262; M. D. Kuhr, "Doubtful Benefits of Tay-Sachs Screening," *New England Journal of Medicine* 292:371, 1975; and by L. Schneck, A. Saifer, and B. W. Volk, "Benefits of Tay-Sachs Screening," *New England Journal of Medicine* 292:758, 1975.

19

Sex Preselection

The medical technology necessary to assure that a baby of a specific gender will be born is already available and is continually being improved. Should such procedures become widespread, the likelihood is that there will be a marked increase in male over female births. A yearning for male babies by prospective parents appears to be manifest in virtually every culture. This is true not only of prospective fathers but of prospective mothers as well. Several studies have revealed that at least two-thirds of all American women express a preference for sons rather than daughters.[1] This desire is even more pronounced among couples planning to have only one child.

The desire to choose the gender of anticipated progeny is certainly a recognizable phenomenon in Jewish culture. "The world cannot exist without males or without females. Happy is he whose children are males and woe unto him whose children are females," declares the Gemara, *Kiddushin* 82b. Whether this dictum reflects a sense of male superiority or simply a pragmatic concern based upon the need to amass a dowry for a daughter, as was the custom in days gone by, is of little importance insofar as the present discussion is concerned. But it should be noted that the halakhic stipulation that a man sire both a son and a daughter in order to conform with the biblical mandate "Be fruitful and multiply" was always sufficient reason for a daughterless father to wish for at least one female child. Clearly, while in the Jewish tradition children of either sex were welcomed as a gift from God, the desire for a child of specific gender was freely expressed without censure.

Even in talmudic times, the desire for children of a particular sex was not simply a subject for wishful thinking. In at least three separate instances the Talmud offers specific advice designed to increase the probability of a male birth. "One who wishes his children to be male and masters of the Torah should examine his actions and woo his wife at the time of intercourse," is the advice of Tractate *Kallah*. Somewhat different advice is offered by the Gemara in *Baba Batra* 10b: "What should a person do so that his children will be males? R. Eliezer says, 'He should gladden his wife prior to intercourse.' " Advice of a similar nature is recorded in *Niddah* 70b-71a in the name of R. Joshua ben Chananiah.

The primary halakhic concern is not with regard to the decision to engage in sex preselection but with the method to be employed in effecting sex determination. The methods to which reference is made in rabbinic literature are hardly the ones recommended by contemporary physicians. In terms of current medical practice the most reliable means of sex preselection is to monitor the fetus by means of amniocentesis or by use of other newly-developed noninvasive methods which reveal the sex of the fetus through analysis of the fluid emitted through the cervix. If it is determined that the fetus is not the desired sex it can then be aborted. It must, however, be emphasized that Jewish teaching unequivocally rejects the option of terminating a pregnancy simply because the fetus is not of the desired sex. Judaism rejects the view that the decision to carry a baby to term or not to do so is a private matter between a woman and her physician. Indeed, Judaism teaches that man lacks proprietary rights with regard to his own body. There is indeed some disagreement with regard to the grounds which would justify an abortion, but no authority would accept sex determination as legitimate cause for an abortion.

Another, less radical, method of sex preselection currently employed involves separation of the androsperm (for males) from the gynosperm (for females). This method presents a different type of problem. The procedure which is utilized for this purpose is essentially the same as the method used for procurement of sperm for purposes of AIH (artificial insemination utilizing the husband's semen). The latter procedure is utilized in order to enable a husband suffering from moderate male infertility to sire children. From the perspective of Jewish law the problem is similar to that of masturbation and onanism. Judaism teaches that the male seed may not be wantonly destroyed. To be sure, the vast majority of rabbinic decisors sanction AIH in order to overcome male infertility provided that proper safeguards are employed against substitution or admixture of the sperm of another male. Any disagreement which exists with regard to AIH is with regard to the proper method to be utilized in the procurement of sperm. The rationale upon which AIH is sanctioned is, however, predicated upon the consideration that such an undertaking is designed to fulfill the commandment "Be fruitful and multiply" and is not at all a form of "wasting" the seed.[2] It must be remembered that in AIH procedures several ejaculations are combined for insemination. The entire ejaculate is deposited in the vagina and no portion of the semen is destroyed. Separation of androsperm from gynosperm is undertaken solely in order to enable insemination with one of the two, but not with both. Thus the procedure, to be effective, must result in the destruction of either the male-producing or the female-producing sperm. Hence, an attempt to determine sex in this manner would be a violation of Jewish law.

A third technique limits intercourse to the period prior, and immediately subsequent, to ovulation. There is some evidence that intercourse during this part of the monthly cycle is more likely to result in a male birth. During this period the ovum is located deep within the genital tract. The length of the migratory path and the extent of the secretions to be traversed are therefore greater. Since male-producing spermatozoa are greater in number and are smaller and hence migrate at a greater speed the statistical probability of a male producing spermatozoa fertilizing the ovum is greater. From the perspective of Jewish law, timing of intercourse is an unobjectionable technique, provided that the wife is willing to forego her claim to conjugal gratification during other periods of the month. In light of the restrictions imposed by the laws of *niddah* this would mean restricting intercourse to one or perhaps two days in the monthly cycle. The likelihood of conceiving a male fetus is enhanced during a four to six-day period prior to ovulation and for a two-day period following ovulation. Restrictions based upon laws of separation during and after the menstrual period effectively bar cohabitation prior to ovulation and usually for a day or so after ovulation as well. It is therefore doubtful that this method would lead to more than a marginal increase in the probability of a male birth.

Assuming that a halakhically non-objectionable technique could be found, there is nevertheless nothing in Jewish law which would *require* a couple to seek to produce a child of either sex. Whatever the operative cultural factors may be, there is certainly no halakhic bias in favor of male children. It is true that the commandment "Be fruitful and multiply" is fulfilled only upon the birth of both a male and a female child. However, a couple who are the parents of any number of children of one sex are under no obligation to utilize any artificial method in order to increase the chance of the birth of a child of the other sex. This is so by virtue of the nature of the *mitzvah* of procreation. The Sages, *Shabbat* 31a, declared that on the day of judgement a person will be asked "Did you engage in procreation?" Note, the individual will not be asked, "Have you sired children?" He will be asked, "*Asakta be-piryah ve-rivyah*—Did you engage in the acts which lead to the birth of children?" This is only logical. Birth is a natural event, an act of God. It does not require a human act, certainly not on the part of the male to whom the *mitzvah* is specifically directed. How, then, can God command a deed which it is not in the power of man to perform? The answer can only be that birth itself is not a *mitzvah;* the *mitzvah* is the act of cohabitation. It is the sexual act which is within the domain of man; what occurs subsequently is in the hands of providence. The birth of a son and a daughter is simply the point at which there is no longer a pentateuchal obligation (as distinct from a continuing obligation stemming from prophetic sources)[3] to continue to perform acts which make procreation possible.

Maimonides, *Hilkhot Ishut* 15:1, makes this point quite clearly. In codifying the *mitzvah* of procreation he is careful to spell out that the *mitzvah* does not constitute an obligation to bear or to sire children but rather, "A man is obligated to engage in coitus at each of the appointed times until he has children."[4] The divine mandate is discharged by engaging in cohabitation with a fertile wife in the normal manner. There is no obligation to seek "heroic measures" to assure the birth of a child, much less so to guarantee the birth of a child of a particular sex.

There are also other considerations auguring against sex

preselection. A society in which human beings are produced according to predetermined specification must reflect to a greater or lesser extent the evils of Huxley's *Brave New World.* There is ample evidence indicating that parents who prefer male children are more numerous than those preferring female progeny. Hence predetermination of sex would undoubtedly lead to a sharp increase in the number of male births. This phenomenon would inherently lead to grave sociological repercussions. A demographic surplus of males over females would mean that a significant number of males would not be able to find marriage partners. Such a situation would certainly be counter to the goals and values of Judaism. It is also quite likely that such a state of affairs would lead to increased prostitution, rape and homosexuality.[5] Jewish teaching would deem such social and moral evils as far too high a price to pay in order to satisfy the desire for progeny of a particular sex.

As a matter of public policy, Jewish law advocates the curbing of even normal sexual activity under certain circumstances. The best example is the admonition found in *Shulchan Arukh, Orach Chaim* 240:12 against cohabitation during periods of hunger. Certainly, tampering with natural processes in a manner which would lead to social upheaval and unrest is contrary to the public policy advocated by Jewish teaching. Assuredly, society would be justified in preventing such a situation from arising. Society would find ample justification in the teachings of Judaism for discouraging widespread sex preselection. Moreover, were sex preselection to become prevalent, society would be justified in demanding the establishment of safeguards in order to assure that the ratio of male to female births remain roughly equal.

NOTES

1. See T. J. Thorndike, "Genetics and the Future of Man," *Horizon,* Autumn 1973, p. 56; Charles F. Westoff and Ronald R. Rindfuss, "Sex Preselection in the United States: Some Implications," *Science,* 184, no. 4137 (May 10, 1974), pp. 633–636; and L. C. Coombs, "Preferences for Sex of Children Among U.S. Couples," *Family Planning Perspectives,* November and December, 1977, p. 259.

2. For a discussion of the halakhic issues involved in artificial insemination see above, chapter 14.

3. "In the morning sow your seed and in the evening withhold not your hand" (Ecclesiastes 11:6) is understood as an exhortation to engage in procreation not only in the "morning" of life, but also in the "evening" of life, i.e., even after statutory requirements have been fulfilled.

4. See also Rabbi Moshe Sternbuch, *Olam ha-Torah,* no. 2 (Tevet-Shevat 5736), pp. 16–23.

5. Amitai Etzioni, "Sex Control, Science and Society," *Science,* 161 (September 13, 1968), pp. 1107–1112.

20

Hazardous Procedures and Experimentation

A clear distinction must be made between medical experimentation which is therapeutic in nature and non-therapeutic experimentation. The former involves procedures of unproven efficacy but is designed to benefit the subject; i.e., should the surgical procedure or experimental drug prove to be of value, the patient will be cured or at least benefited thereby. The moral problem arises in cases in which the procedure is dangerous to the life of the patient; e.g., the drug prescribed for the treatment of an illness may have toxic side effects. The question of whether, and under what conditions, risks may legitimately be assumed by the patient requires clarification.

It goes without saying that the patient is under no *obligation* to assume the risks involved in hazardous experimentation. In fact, at least one authority rules that although the patient must seek medical treatment, he need not make use of experimental procedures even if they involve no inherent risk.

As has been shown in the first chapter, a patient, according to Jewish law, may be compelled to submit to medically indicated therapy. However, declares Rabbi Jacob Emden *(Mor u-Ketziah, Orach Chaim* 328), a distinction must be made between therapeutic procedures of proven efficacy and those of unproven therapeutic value. Acceptance of a therapeutic procedure of known efficacy, known as a *refuah bedukah,* is a moral and halakhic imperative. The patient may not terminate or shorten his life, either actively or passively. Since God grants dispensation to seek medical cure, use of medicaments or acceptance of other forms of therapy in such situations is mandatory. Man may no more abstain from the use of drugs to cure illness than he may abstain from food and drink. However, if the proposed therapy is of unproven value the patient may legitimately refuse treatment. This is true not only when the treatment itself is potentially hazardous, but even if there is no reason to suspect that the proposed treatment may be harmful in any way. When the proposed therapy is experimental in nature, use of such treatment is discretionary; the patient may legitimately decline treatment and rely exclusively upon divine providence. Thus, the patient may decline a drug or procedure whose curative powers are questionable. This is not to say that a moral obligation to seek a cure exists only if the physician is in a position to guarantee with certainty that a recovery will ensue. The examples given of demonstrable efficacy, viz., amputation of a limb, application of salves and bandages, certainly are not of absolute curative power. Despite the most attentive medical ministrations, some patients do not recover. However, the procedures enumerated are of known value in treating certain afflictions and hence must be pursued. Nevertheless, drugs or surgical procedures whose causal efficacy has not been demonstrated may be rejected by the patient. Experimental procedures, including those which are non-hazardous in nature, certainly fall within this category.

The distinction between a *refuah bedukah* and a *refuah she-einah bedukah* may best be understood in light of the previously presented philosophical considerations inherent in the obligation to heal. As God's creature, governed by divine providence, man is fundamentally expected to place his faith and trust in God. In instructing Adam to eat of the fruit of all trees in the Garden of Eden save the Tree of Knowledge, God reveals to man that the bounty of the universe has been placed at man's disposal. Man is denied the right to refuse to partake of food on the plea that God will provide for him. God has, in effect, told Adam that providence in its most basic form is manifest in the natural order. Food has been placed in the universe for man's benefit. Man is expected to make use of food and drink in order to sustain life. Failure to do so is tantamount to suicide and constitutes flaunting the will of God.

Certainly, a person finding himself marooned on a desert

island is obligated to make use of whatever food is available in order to sustain life. But finding no food, is he obliged to eat grass or chips of wood in an attempt to ward off death? It seems obvious that while the person may valiantly attempt to obtain nourishment from such sources, if he should so desire, there nevertheless exists no obligation for him to do so. This would be true even in the absence of evidence demonstrating that such materials provide no nutrition for man. God demands of man that he sustain life and concomitantly makes known to man in a positive manner ways in which life may be sustained. Adam is told that God has providentially provided fruit trees for his sustenance. When, and if, divine providence enables man to develop the scientific technology necessary to extract nutrients from cellulose, this will be clear indication to man that God wishes him to utilize such measures, if necessary, in order to preserve life. In the absence of such knowledge man may, if he desires, revert to a pristine reliance upon God.

Precisely the same is true with regard to pharmaceutical means of sustaining life. When God enables man to discover a causal connection between a drug and the cure of a disease, man has no right to ignore the available therapy and to turn directly to God instead. Such a posture involves contravention of the divine will. Yet, in the absence of a known cure, a person afflicted by disease is under no obligation to visit an apothecary's shop and request a dose of every medicine in stock in the hope that perhaps one of the drugs available will be of some help. God demands only that man avail himself of drugs possessing known medicinal qualities, just as he demands only that vegetation of known nutritive value be used as food. The absence of an awareness of an effective remedy is an indication that God does not *demand* of man that he seek a cure for such an affliction. Man is at perfect liberty to utilize an experimental remedy if he so chooses. But since no obligation to do so has been imposed upon him, a person finding himself in such circumstances is equally free to surrender himself entirely to the will of God.

It is a principle of Jewish law that the obligation to cure and to preserve life is not limited to situations in which it may be anticipated that subsequent to therapy the patient will have a normal life expectancy. As noted, the Talmud, *Yoma* 85a, clearly indicates that a victim trapped under the debris of a fallen wall is to be rescued even if as a result of such efforts his life will be prolonged only by a matter of moments. Not only is every human life of infinite value, but every moment of human life is of infinite value. Accordingly, ritual restrictions such as Sabbath laws are suspended even for the most minimal prolongation of life.

Despite the sanctity with which every moment of life is endowed, it is at times permissible to accept therapy which, if ineffective, may foreshorten life. When minimal duration of life *(chayyei sha'ah)* is weighed against the possibility of cure accompanied by normal life expectancy, Jewish teaching accepts the principle that reasonable risks may be incurred in order to effect a recovery. Thus, hazardous procedures may be resorted to despite the fact that the proposed therapy is of a nature that the drug or procedure may prove to be ineffective and the patient's life shortened thereby. This principle may be derived from the talmudic discussion recorded in *Avodah Zarah* 27b concerning the incident of the four leprous men described in II Kings 7:3–4. The Syrian army had besieged Samaria. In addition, the region was suffering under a great famine. The lepers recognized that if they took no action they would die of hunger in a relatively short period of time. Were they, however, to cross into the Syrian lines, one of two things would happen: either they would immediately be put to death as enemies or, if pitied because of their infirmity, they would be provided with food and their lives saved. Despite the danger, they reasoned, "Now therefore come, and let us fall into the host of the Syrians; if they save us alive, we shall live; and if they kill us, we shall but die." The Talmud views this narrative as providing scriptural sanction for the risk of immediate death in an attempt to restore conditions necessary for normal life expectancy. Based upon this talmudic discussion,[1] numerous rabbinic authorities specifically permit use of a hazardous drug which might cause death to result "within an hour or two " on behalf of a patient who would otherwise have lived for "a day or two days." Despite the brevity of the period of time which the patient might be expected to live without therapy, these authorities mandate consultation with "proficient medical specialists of the city" and rule that hazardous therapy may be instituted only if the physicians recommend it by at least a majority of two to one. Nevertheless, even when recommended by competent physicians, procedures which involve a significant risk of shortening life are discretionary rather than mandatory.

A related problem is the attitude toward hazardous therapy for alleviation of pain or other symptoms rather than for the cure of a potentially fatal illness. The permissibility of placing one's life in danger when not afflicted by a life-threatening malady requires justification. The great value placed upon preservation of life augurs against placing oneself in a risk situation. In general, Jewish law teaches that man may not expose himself to danger. An entire section of the Code of Law (*Yoreh De'ah* 116) is devoted to an enumeration of actions and situations which must be avoided because they present an element of risk. One hypothesis which may be advanced in sanctioning risks undertaken in a medical context is that the verse "And he shall cause him to be thoroughly healed" grants blanket dispensation for any sound medical practice. Nachmanides[2] and Rabbenu Nissim Gerondi[3] both comment that all modes of therapy are potentially dangerous. In the words of Rabbenu Nissim, "All modes of therapy are a danger for the patient, for it is possible that if the physician errs with regard to a specific drug, it will kill the patient." Nachmanides states even more explicitly, "With regard to cures, there is naught but danger; what heals one kills another." Nevertheless, healing—even of non life-threatening afflictions—is sanctioned by Scripture. Apparently then, since every therapy is fraught with danger, the hazards of treatment are specifically sanctioned as constituting a morally acceptable risk when incurred in conjunction with a therapeutic protocol. Accordingly, the practice of the healing arts, despite the hazards involved, cannot be branded as sinful even if designed simply for the alleviation of pain.[4]

Utilization of medical procedures which are ordinary and usual but which carry with them an element of risk may be justified on other grounds as well. The Talmud, in a variety of instances, indicates that a person may engage in commonplace activities even though he places himself in a position of danger in doing so. In justifying such conduct the Talmud declares, "Since many have trodden thereon, 'the Lord preserveth the simple' " (Psalms 116:6).[5] The principle enunciated in this dictum is that man is justified in placing his trust in God provided that the risk involved is of a type which is commonly accepted as a reasonable one by society at large. It may readily be argued that any accepted therapeutic procedure may be classified in this manner.

Hazardous non-therapeutic medical experimentation involving human subjects poses an entirely different moral problem. Such experiments are unlikely to be of benefit to the patient himself, but may yield valuable information which may be of great benefit to other patients in the future. Such a situation presents a crucial problem, viz., may a person place his life in jeopardy in order to save another? Man does not exercise proprietorship over his own body and, hence, may not sacrifice it in order to spare another.[6] The principle, "Why do you think that your blood is sweeter than your friend's?" is the talmudic rationale which proscribes saving one's life at the cost of the life of another. The same principle in reverse, viz., "Why do you think that the blood of your friend is sweeter than yours?" precludes the sacrifice of one's own life in order to save that of another.

But what of situations in which, while there does exist some danger to one's own life, the loss of one's own life is merely possible, but not certain, whereas the rescue of one's fellow man is certain? The answer to this question is important not only in order to establish the teaching of Judaism with regard to non-therapeutic experimentation, but also with regard to organ transplants involving living donors. This question will therefore by analyzed in Chapter 23 in conjunction with our discussion of transplant surgery.

NOTES

1. R. Meir Posner, *Bet Meir, Yoreh De'ah* 339:1, and R. Jacob Reischer, *Shevut Ya'akov,* III, no. 85.

2. *Torat ha Adam* in *Kitvei Ramban,* ed. Bernard Chavel (Jerusalem, 5724), II, 43.

3. Commentary on *Sanhedrin* 84b.

4. Cf. R. Jacob Emden, *Mor u-Ketzi'ah* 328, and R. Eli'ezer Waldenberg, *Tzitz Eli'ezer,* X, no. 25, chap. 17, sec. 5.

5. *Shabbat* 129b and *Niddah* 31a.

6. Possible exceptions are saving the life of a child by a parent or rescue of a great Torah scholar. See *Tzitz Eli'ezer,* IX, *maftechot,* no. 45. Cf. however, R. Zevi Hirsch Meisels, *Teshuvot Mekadshei ha-Shem,* I, *Sha'ar Machmadim,* pp. 9–10. Another exception, preservation of the entire community of Israel, is discussed by R. Abraham I. Kook, *Mishpat Kohen,* no. 144, sec. 17.

21

Animal Experiments

Jewish law is replete with regulations designed to protect the well-being of animals. Thus the Bible commands, "You shall not muzzle the ox when he treads out the corn" (Deuteronomy 25:4). Placing the ox in close proximity to corn but preventing him from partaking of the food he treads upon is untoward cruelty. Similarly, a person is obligated to provide food for domestic animals before himself sitting down to a meal. For similar reasons, an animal may not be overworked.[1] In general, infliction of cruelty upon animals constitutes a biblical offense.[2]

Despite these strictures against cruelty toward animals, Judaism knows nothing of anti-vivisection statutes which serve to bar animal experimentation. Animals were created for the benefit of men and may be used for food and as beasts of burden. Vegetarianism is thus not generally regarded as a form of exemplary piety. Animals may be used for other purposes as well, even though utilization for such purposes results in incidental pain to the animal, e.g., feathers may be removed for use as quills.

The fundamental criterion establishing a line of demarcation between the permissible and the forbidden is the relationship of the act involved to a legitimate human need. Cruelty for its own sake or for the sake of sport is always forbidden. Rabbinic authorities have ruled that hunting as a sport is forbidden for precisely this reason.[3] Scientific experiments upon laboratory animals designed to yield information of potential benefit to mankind are sanctioned by Jewish law as legitimate utilization of animals for the tangible benefit of mankind. Of course, pain may be inflicted upon the animal only to the degree absolutely necessary in order to obtain the required information. Otherwise, the pain does not serve to satisfy a legitimate need and is prohibited. It should be stressed that this criterion is a pragmatic one: The benefits must be practical in nature and not simply the satisfaction of intellectual curiosity. Thus, while animal research by scientists is justified, and while surgical skills may be perfected by practice upon animals, it is difficult to find grounds which would permit a teacher to demand that a student perform experiments which inflict pain upon animals unless the experiment is directly related to the development of a specific skill necessary for fulfillment of the student's professional or vocational goal.

Castration, spaying, or sterilization of animals is forbidden under all circumstances. Emasculation of animals is prohibited on the basis of the verse, "And that which is mauled or crushed or torn or cut you shall not offer unto the Lord; nor shall you do this in your land" (Leviticus 22:34).

The Jewish attitude toward causing pain to animals even when not specifically prohibited is eloquently reflected in the following talmudic anecdote.[4] Once a calf was being led to slaughter and passed in front of Rabbi Judah the Prince, the compiler of the Mishnah. The calf ran to Rabbi Judah and burying its head in his cloak began to bleat, as if imploring him to intercede on its behalf. Rabbi Judah reacted by exclaiming, "Go; for this purpose were you created!" Rabbi Judah received a heavenly punishment for his lack of compassion and suffered severe pain for a period of thirteen years. Thirteen years later, Rabbi Judah's servant was sweeping the house and coming upon a number of small animals made a motion indicating that she was about to kill them. Rabbi Judah exclaimed, "Leave them alone, for it is written, 'And God's mercy extends over all His creatures' " (Psalms 145:9). In Heaven it was proclaimed, "Since he is merciful, let us have mercy on him." Only after showing mercy to the animal was Rabbi Judah relieved from suffering.

NOTES

1. *Choshen Mishpat* 272:1.
2. *Choshen Mishpat* 272:9.
3. *Shemesh Tzedakah, Yoreh De'ah,* nos. 18 and 57; cf. *Noda bi-Yehudah,* II, *Yoreh De'ah,* no. 10. For further sources regarding the rabbinic view toward hunting, see *Va-Yikra Rabbah* 13:3; *Teshuvot Maharam Rothenberg,* no. 27; *Or Zaru'a,* II, 19a; *Pachad Yitzchak,* s.v. *Tzeidah; Levush, Orach Chaim* 316:2; Rema, *Orach Chaim* 316:2; *Givat Sha'ul,* pp. 87–88; and *Darkei Teshuvah, Yoreh De'ah* 117:44.
4. *Baba Metzi'a* 85a.

22

Plastic Surgery

As have been stated earlier, Judaism recognizes divine proprietorship over all objects of creation, including the human body. Judaism expressly teaches that the individual has no proprietary rights with regard to his own body (See Rambam, *Hilkhot Chovel u-Mazik* 5:1). A person's body is committed to him for safekeeping, and hence self-mutilation or any form of assault upon the body is viewed as a breach of this stewardship. Dispensation for intervention in physiological processes for therapeutic purposes is granted in the biblical directive, "And he shall cause him to be thoroughly healed" (Exodus 21:19). Thus, a surgical operation to correct a deformed or malfunctioning organ is specifically excluded from the prohibition against "wounding."

Perfection of highly sophisticated medical techniques has led to the development of a wide range of elective surgical procedures. As a result, cosmetic surgery is becoming increasingly more commonplace in our society. From the perspective of Halakhah, elective plastic surgery undertaken solely for cosmetic or aesthetic purposes differs significantly from other corrective procedures. The obvious halakhic problem associated with plastic surgery is whether or not such procedures involve infractions of the law against wounding *(chavalah)*. A further, more general, question is raised by the risk to life involved in such procedures. Any form of surgery, particularly when performed under general anesthesia, poses at least a minimal, but nevertheless significant, threat to life. Is it permissible according to Halakhah to expose oneself to such danger for cosmetic purposes? A third question is posed by cosmetic surgery performed upon male patients. The prohibition "A man shall not put on a woman's garment" (Deuteronomy 22:5) extends not only to the wearing of female clothing by a male but also to the application of cosmetics or to any act of beautification usually associated with women. Dyeing of the hair and removal of armpit or pubic hair are specifically enumerated acts of this nature. Are such forms of plastic surgery as face-lifting, nasoplasty, etc., so widely associated with women as to constitute a form of "female dress," or may men avail themselves of such methods for purposes of improving their appearance?

As has been demonstrated in an earlier chapter, "wounding" is permissible not only for curing a physiological disorder but also for purposes of alleviating pain. *Shulchan Arukh, Yoreh De'ah* 241:3, states that a son should not "wound" his father even for medical reasons. Hence, he should not remove a splinter, perform bloodletting or amputate a limb. Rema adds that if no other physician is available and the father is "in pain" the son may perform bloodletting or an amputation on behalf of his father. A similar statement is made by Me'iri, *Sanhedrin* 84b. Since the phraseology employed by these sources indicates that the contemplated procedures were designed to mitigate pain rather than to effect a cure, it may be concluded that alleviation of pain is included in the pronouncement "And he shall surely heal" and hence excluded from the prohibition against "wounding."

The halakhic definition of pain is significantly expanded by *Tosafot, Shabbat* 50b. *Tosafot* states that a state of mind which prevents a person from mingling with people constitutes "pain" within the halakhic definition of that term. Accordingly, if an individual shuns normal social intercourse as a result of a deformity or other disfigurement, the condition causing distress may be corrected by means of plastic surgery.

Plastic surgery designed to rectify conditions as a result of which the afflicted individual experiences difficulty in finding employment or a marriage partner presents a somewhat different problem. *Tosafot, Baba Kamma* 91b, clearly states that "wounding" is forbidden even when undertaken for purposes of pecuniary advantage. Quite obviously, the desire for financial gain is not in itself sufficient grounds upon which to justify "wounding." Nevertheless, it would appear that the psychological anguish normally attendant upon not being able to find gainful employment or a suitable marriage partner is a form of "pain" no less severe than distress at not feeling free to mingle socially with other people. It would follow that in such circumstances cosmetic surgery is permissible in order to alleviate this anguish.[1]

Cosmetic surgery, when permissible, is permissible not only for women but for men as well. As has been indicated, cosmetic surgery is not permitted simply for purposes of beautification but is sanctioned in order to alleviate psychological anguish. *Tosafot, Shabbat* 50b, states that males are permitted to use cosmetics if such cosmetics are applied for purposes of alleviating pain. It follows, therefore, that other forms of beautification commonly associated with women are also permitted to males, provided they are designed primarily for purposes of alleviating pain. Moreover, in our society, cosmetic surgery is not a uniquely feminine form of beautification but is widely practiced by males as well and, accordingly, does not constitute an infraction of the prohibition against the wearing of female garments.[2]

NOTES

1. See R. Ya'akov Breisch, *Chelkat Ya'akov,* III, no. 11; R. Eli'ezer Waldenberg, *Tzitz Eli'ezer,* XI, no. 4; and R. Menasheh Klein, *Mishneh Halakhot,* IV, no. 246.
2. *Chelkat Ya'akov,* III, no. 11, and *Mishneh Halakhot* IV, no. 247.

23

Organ Transplants

The most significant question posed in consideration of whether or not organ transplants are permissible is the justification of the hazard to which the donor is subjected in such procedures. Is a person obligated, or even permitted, to place his life in danger in order to preserve the life of his fellow-man? A number of authorities record a view attributed to the Palestinian Talmud which *requires* a person to jeopardize (but not sacrifice—as stated earlier) his life in order to save his fellow. R. Joseph Karo amplifies this position by stating that it is predicated upon the reasoning that "certainty" takes precedence over "possibility" (*Bet Yosef, Choshen Mishpat* 426). The effect of this rationale is to limit the obligation posited by the Palestinian Talmud to situations in which it is justified to assume that the procedure will *certainly* save the life of the beneficiary.

However, the requirement to risk one's life in order to save the life of another is not cited in any of the codes of Jewish law. This has led a number of rabbinic authorities to advance arguments designed to demonstrate that the Babylonian Talmud differs with the Palestinian Talmud and posits no such requirement. Accordingly, most authorities do not regard the jeopardization of one's own life to be obligatory. Yet, while at least one scholar, R. David ibn Zimra (16th cent.), considers one who does so to be a "pious fool,"[1] the assumption of such a risk cannot be considered a transgression. The matter is best summed up in the words of Rabbi Yechiel Michal Epstein, author of an early twentieth-century compendium, *Arukh ha-Shulchan,* who, paraphrasing an earlier source, writes, "However, everything depends upon the circumstances; it is necessary to weigh the matter on a scale and not to safeguard oneself more than necessary."[2]

It would appear that the question of hazardous experiments which have no anticipated therapeutic benefit to the subject can be analyzed in much the same manner. There is no obligation to volunteer for such hazards; yet, although an individual subjecting himself to such risks may perhaps be a "pious fool," the person doing so commits no transgression.[3] It is unconscionable, and a violation of Jewish law, to subject a person to such hazards without fully apprising him of all possible risks and obtaining his informed consent. Moreover, the risk is warranted only if it is anticipated that information derived from the experimentation will be of value in the treatment of a *choleh le-faneinu,* a patient already afflicted by a disease or physiological disorder. This concept was first articulated by R. Ezekiel Landau of Prague in the eighteenth century in his celebrated responsum on autopsies, which will be examined in a later chapter. This concept was understood by a renowned twentieth-century scholar, R. Abraham I. Karelitz (popularly known as *Chazon Ish*), to include potential victims of a plague or epidemic[4] and applied by Rabbi I. Y. Unterman to battlefield situations in permitting the erection and supplying of field hospitals on the Sabbath even prior to the firing of the first shot.[5] The reasoning is that epidemics invariably claim victims and war situations forebode casualties.

Let us return to the question of organ transplants. Although, as we have seen, it is permissible to assume risks in order to save the life of another, there is no obligation to donate a limb or organ for this purpose. There are strong grounds for arguing that, even according to the view attributed to the Palestinian Talmud, there is no obligation to sacrifice an organ. To subject oneself to danger from which one may emerge unscathed is one thing; to sacrifice a limb or an organ which will not under any circumstances be regenerated is quite another. A person may avail himself of property belonging to another in order to save his own life, but with the anticipation of making restitution at some future time. Insofar as organs are concerned this is patently impossible. R. David ibn Zimra adds that it is inconceivable that the Torah, "whose paths are paths of pleasantness"

(Proverbs 8:17), would *demand* such a great sacrifice of any person as a matter of *obligation*. Nevertheless, a person who donates an organ in order to save the life of another has clearly performed an act of *chesed* (loving-kindness) of the highest order.

Heart transplants do not pose novel theoretical problems of substance. To be sure, in a celebrated controversy, two renowned authorities, R. Zevi Ashkenazi[6] and R. Jonathan Eibeschutz,[7] disagreed over the possibility of a chicken existing and growing to maturity without a heart. But R. Zevi Ashkenazi's statement that a creature cannot live without a heart does not refer to a chicken attached to a heart-lung machine. There is no reason to conclude that he would have considered the removal of the recipient's diseased heart while the recipient is attached to a heart-lung machine to be an act of murder. If this were the case, then implantation of a new heart would be tantamount to resurrection of the dead! By the same token, all open-heart surgery involving the stopping of the heart in order to provide a stationary field for surgery, while the functions of the heart are taken over by a heart-lung machine, would be tantamount to murder.

Opposition in rabbinic circles to heart transplants is based upon two considerations: (1) On occasion, the donor's heart has been removed before it has stopped beating. According to Jewish law, the donor is still alive and removal of the beating heart constitutes an act of homicide. Furthermore, a *goses* (moribund person) may not be moved for fear of hastening his death. Accordingly, even preparations for transplant surgery, such as wheeling the donor to an operating theater, etc., would be forbidden while the donor is yet alive. (2) The probability of success is considered to be extremely slim. It is the opinion of many authorities that, at least at the present time, the hazards to the recipient are too great to warrant the risks involved.

Cadaver transplants and the permissibility of willing one's organs pose a different set of problems. The considerations with regard to these questions are closely akin to those posed by autopsies. These questions will be examined in a later chapter. As will be shown, post-mortem examinations are permissible when designed to yield information necessary to remove an already existing threat to life. Transplantation of an organ from a corpse to a living recipient is similarly permissible if necessary in order to eliminate a danger to the life of the recipient.

Renal disease constitutes an immediate threat to the life of the patient. Transplantation of a healthy kidney to replace the non-functioning kidneys of the patient is permissible. Kidney transplants are permissible even though accumulated body wastes may be eliminated by dialysis involving intermittent use of an artificial kidney since the general prognosis for the patient following a successful kidney transplant is more favorable than for the patient treated by dialysis. As stated earlier, cadaver transplants are permitted only if the kidney is removed after the donor has been pronounced dead in accordance with the criteria of Jewish law and unwarranted procedures are not performed while the donor is yet in a state of *gesisah.* Thus, the moribund patient may not be moved, nor may other procedures be initiated, until death has actually taken place.

It is the consensus of rabbinic opinion that eye or corneal transplants are permissible provided that the patient is blind in both eyes. Bilateral blindness constitutes danger to the life of the totally blind person since he cannot perceive danger and is in constant danger of falling, slipping, or colliding with objects which may endanger his life. A transplant designed to restore sight is thus a matter of *pikuach nefesh* (saving a life). Some, but by no means all, authorities permit a corneal transplant on behalf of a patient who is blind in only one eye.[8] Competent rabbinic advice should be sought in every individual case.

These statements apply only to removal of organs from a cadaver for purposes of immediate implantation in a recipient in need of the transplant. Removal of an organ for storage in an organ bank presents a different problem which will be analyzed in our discussion of autopsies.

NOTES

1. *Teshuvot Radbaz,* III, no. 627.
2. *Choshen Mishpat* 426:4.
3. Cf. however, R. Eli'ezer Waldenberg, *Tzitz Eli'ezer,* IX, no. 45, sec. 13.

4. *Chazon Ish, Oholot* 22:32.

5. *Torah she-be-al Peh,* XI (5729), 14. Cf. R. Shlomo Goren, *Shevilin,* Iyar 5729, pp. 22–24.

6. *Teshuvot Chakham Zevi,* no. 74.

7. *Kereti u-Peleti* 40:4.

8. See Rabbi I. Y. Unterman, *Shevet me-Yehudah,* I, 313 ff., and R. Yekutiel Yehudah Greenwald, *Kol Bo al Avelut,* pp. 45–47.

24

Euthanasia

Until relatively recently, medical science offered all or nothing in its treatment of virtually all illnesses and defects. Either the patient responded to treatment, when treatment was available, and was cured, or else he succumbed as a result of his malady. Such dichotomous situations generated few moral dilemmas for the medical practitioner. Patients, by and large, sought treatment and physicians strained to do all that was in their power in order to effect a cure. To be sure, theologians and ethicists agonized over such questions as the moral legitimacy of euthanasia for patients who found continued existence too painful to bear and the extent to which the patient was obliged to seek extraordinary means in effecting a cure; but the number of people with regard to whom such perplexities were germane was rather small.

In recent years medical science and technology have made tremendous strides. Some diseases have been virtually eradicated; for others, effective remedies have been found. Concomitantly, ways and means have been developed which enable physicians to sustain life even when known cures do not exist. While heretofore untreatable conditions now respond to medical ministrations, such response is often less than total. In such cases, questions with regard to the value of the life which is preserved become very real.

The physician's practical dilemma can be stated in simple terms: to treat or not to treat. In deciding whether or not to initiate or maintain such treatment, the physician is called upon to make not only medical, but also moral determinations. There are at least two distinguishable components which present themselves in all such quandaries. The first is a value judgment. Is it desirable that the patient be treated? Should value judgments be made with regard to the quality of life to be preserved? The second question pertains to the personal responsibilities of the physician and of the patient. Under what circumstances, and to what extent, is the physician morally obligated to persist in rendering aggressive professional care? Is the patient always obliged to seek treatment for prolonging of life even though a cure is not anticipated?

Jewish teaching with regard to these questions is shaped by the earlier-stated belief that not only is human life in general of infinite and inestimable value, but that every moment of life is of infinite value as well. Accordingly, obligations with regard to treatment and cure are one and the same, whether the person's life is likely to be prolonged for a matter of years or merely for a few seconds. An exception is made only for the case of a person in a state of *gesisah,* i.e., a moribund patient (as defined by Halakhah) in whom the death process has actually begun. Thus, even on the Sabbath, efforts to free a victim buried under a collapsed building must be continued even if the victim is found in such circumstances that he cannot survive longer than a brief period of time.[1] Sectarians such as the Sadducees, who lived during the period of the Second Commonwealth, and the Karaites of the Geonic period, who challenged these provisions of Jewish law and, by implication, the value system upon which they are predicated, were branded heretics.[2]

Life with suffering is regarded as being, in many cases, preferable to cessation of life and with it elimination of suffering. The Talmud, *Sotah* 22a, and Maimonides, *Hilkhot Sotah* 3:20, indicate that the adulterous woman who was made to drink "the bitter waters" (Numbers 6:11–31) did not always die immediately. If she possessed other merit, though guilty of the offense with which she was charged, the waters, rather than causing her to perish immediately, produced a debilitating and degenerative state which led to a protracted termination of life. The added longevity, although accompanied by pain and suffering, is viewed as a privilege bestowed in recognition of meritorious actions. Life accompanied by pain is thus viewed as preferable to death. It is this sentiment which is reflected in the words of the Psalmist, "The Lord has indeed chastened me, but He has not left me to die" (Psalms 118:18).

The practice of euthanasia—whether active or passive—is contrary to the teachings of Judaism. Any positive act designed to hasten the death of the patient is equated with murder in Jewish law, even if death is hastened only by a matter of moments. No matter how laudable the intentions of the person performing an act of mercy-killing may be, his deed constitutes an act of homicide.

"But your blood of your lives will I require; from the hand of every beast will I require it; and from the hand of man, from the hand of a person's brother, will I require the life of man" (Genesis 9:5). This detailed biblical prohibition against homicide contains one phrase which is an apparent redundancy. Since the phrase "from the hand of man" pronounces man culpable for the murder of his fellow-man, to what point is it necessary for Scripture to reiterate "from the hand of a person's brother will I require the life of man"? Fratricide is certainly no less heinous a crime than ordinary homicide. R. Ya'akov Zevi Mecklenburg, in his commentary on the Pentateuch, *Ha-Ketav ve-ha-Kabbalah,* astutely comments that while murder is the antithesis of brotherly love, in some circumstances the taking of the life of one's fellow-man may be perceived as indeed being an act of love par excellence. Euthanasia, designed to put an end to unbearable suffering, is born not of hatred or anger, but of concern and compassion. It is precisely the taking of life, even under circumstances in which it is manifestly obvious that the perpetrator is motivated by feelings of love and brotherly compassion, which the Torah finds necessary to brand as murder, pure and simple. Despite the noble intent which prompts such an action, mercy-killing is proscribed as an unwarranted intervention in an area which must be governed only by God Himself. The life of man may be reclaimed only by the Author of life. As long as man is yet endowed with a spark of life—as defined by God's eternal law—man dare not presume to hasten death, no matter how hopeless or meaningless continued existence may appear to be in the eyes of a mortal perceiver.

Jewish law with regard to care of the dying is spelled out

with care and precision. The terminal patient, even when he is a *goses,* i.e., a person who has become moribund and whose death is imminent, is regarded as a living person in every respect. One must not pry his jaws, anoint him, wash him, plug his orifices, remove the pillow from underneath him or place him on the ground.[3] It is also forbidden to close his eyes "for whoever closes the eyes with the onset of death is a shedder of blood."[4] Each of these acts is forbidden because the slightest movement of the patient may hasten death. As the Talmud puts it, "The matter may be compared to a flickering flame; as soon as one touches it, the light is extinguished."[5] Accordingly, any movement or manipulation of the dying person is forbidden.

Passive euthanasia involving the omission of a therapeutic procedure, or the withholding of medication, which could sustain life is also prohibited by Jewish law. The terminal nature of an illness in no way mitigates the physician's responsibilities. The physician is charged with prolonging life no less than with effecting a cure.

Elimination of pain is certainly a legitimate and laudable goal. According to some authorities it is encompassed within the general obligation to heal;[6] it is certainly mandated by virtue of the commandment "Love thy neighbor as thyself." Yet when the dual goals of avoidance of pain and preservation of life come into conflict with one another, Judaism recognizes the paramount value and sanctity of life and, accordingly, assigns priority to preservation of life. Thus, a number of authorities have expressly stated that non-treatment or withdrawal of treatment in order for the patient to be freed from pain by death constitutes euthanasia and is not countenanced by Judaism.[7] This remains the case even if the patient himself pleads to be permitted to die. As stated by one prominent authority, "Even if the patient himself cries out, 'Leave me be and do not give me any aid because for me death is preferable' " everything possible must be done on behalf of the patient.[8]

Nevertheless, everything possible should be done to alleviate the patient's suffering. This includes aggressive treatment of pain even to a degree which at present is not common in medical practice. Physicians are reluctant to use morphine in high dosages because of the danger of depression of the cerebral center responsible for respiration. The effect of such medications is that the patient cannot control the muscles necessary for breathing. There is, however, no halakhic objection to providing such medication in order to control pain in the case of terminal patients and maintaining such patients on a respirator. Similarly, there is no halakhic objection to the use of heroin in the control of pain in terminal patients. The danger of addiction under such circumstances is, of course, hardly a significant consideration. At present, the use of heroin is illegal even for medical purposes. Judaism firmly believes that everything in creation is designed for a purpose. Alleviation of otherwise intractable pain is a known beneficial use of heroin. Marijuana is effective in alleviating nausea which is a side-effect of some forms of chemotherapy. There is every reason to believe that these drugs were given to man for the specific purpose of controlling pain and discomfort. Jewish teaching would enthusiastically endorse legislation legalizing the use—with adequate accompanying safeguards—of these substances in the treatment of terminal patients.

In discharging his responsibility with regard to prolongation of life the physician must make use of any medical resources which are available. However, as shown earlier, he is not obligated to employ procedures which are themselves hazardous in nature and may potentially foreshorten the life of the patient. Nor is either the physician or the patient obligated to employ a therapy which is experimental in nature.

Jewish law, however, makes no distinction between "natural means," such as food or drink, and artificial means, such as drugs and medications. Rambam in his *Commentary on the Mishnah, Pesachim* 4:9, draws a cogent parallel between food and medication. God created food and water; we are obliged to use them in staving off hunger and thirst. God created drugs and medicaments and endowed man with the intelligence necessary to discover their medicinal properties; we are obliged to use them in warding off illness and disease. Similarly, God provided the materials and the technology which make possible catheters, intravenous infusions, and respirators; we are obligated to use them in order to prolong life.

Medication, therefore, may not be withheld from an incurable patient. Thus, for example, insulin may not be withheld from a diabetic who suffers from debilitating terminal illness in order to hasten his demise. By the same token, Jewish law recognizes no distinction between "ordinary" and "extraordinary" modes of therapy. The obligation to preserve and prolong life requires the use of any available mode of therapy, subject to the limitations which have been discussed. Indeed, terms such as "extraordinary means" and "heroic measures" are alien to the vocabulary of rabbinic literature.

For these same reasons, Judaism cannot sanction a "living will" or the provisions of legislation such as the Natural Death Acts which have been enacted by a number of state legislatures. Such legislation is designed to bind the physician to respect the wishes of the patient and, under certain conditions, to withhold or withdraw life-sustaining procedures in the event of a terminal malady. Judaism denies man the right to make judgments with regard to quality of life. The category of *pikuach nefesh* extends to human life of every description, including the feeble-minded, the mentally deranged, and even persons in a so-called vegetative state. The *mitzvah* of saving a life is neither enhanced nor diminished by virtue of the quality of life preserved. Nor, in the final analysis, does the desire of the patient to have, or not to have, his life prolonged play a role in the halakhic obligation to initiate or maintain life-sustaining procedures.

Judaism does not perceive the overriding obligation to preserve life to be in any way antithetical to "death with dignity." It is Judaism which teaches that the human body must be accorded every sign of dignity in death as well as in life. But the struggle for life is never an indignity. The attempt to sustain life, by whatever means, is naught but the expression of the highest regard for the precious nature of the gift of life and of the dignity in which it is held.

It is quite true that man has the power to prolong life far beyond the point at which it ceases to be either productive or pleasurable. Not infrequently, the patient, if capable of expressing his desires and allowed to follow his own inclinations, would opt for termination of a life which has become a burden both to others and to himself. Judaism, however, teaches that man does not enjoy the right of self-determination with regard to questions of life and death. Generations ago our Sages wrote, "Against your will you live; against your will you die."[9] While conventionally understood as underscoring the irony that a baby wishes to be born no more than an adult wishes to die, these words today take on new meaning. They may be taken quite literally as an eloquent summary of the Jewish view with regard to both euthanasia and the withholding of life-sustaining treatment. Judaism has always taught that life, no less than death, is involuntary. Only the Creator, who bestows the gift of life, may relieve man of that life, even when it has become a burden rather than a blessing.

Although euthanasia in any form is forbidden, and the hastening of death, even by a matter of moments, is regarded as tantamount to murder, there is one situation in which treatment may be withheld from the moribund patient in order to provide for an unimpeded death. While the death of a *goses* may not be hastened, there is no obligation to perform any action which will lengthen the life of the patient in this state. The distinction between an active and a passive act applies to a *goses* and to a *goses* only. When a patient is, as it were, actually in the clutches of the angel of death and the death process has actually begun, there is no obligation to heal. Therefore, Rema permits the removal of "anything which constitutes a hindrance to the departure of the soul, such as a clattering noise or salt upon his tongue . . . since such acts involve no active hastening of death, but only the removal of the impediment."[10] Some authorities not only sanction withholding of treatment but prohibit any action which may prolong the agony of a *goses.*[11] Other authorities (*Bi'ur Halakhah, Orach Chaim* 329:2, and Rabbi Eliezer Waldenberg, *Ramat Rachel,* no. 28) insist that the life of a *goses* may not be shortened even passively by withdrawal of medication. They apparently are of the opinion that withholding of medical therapy is not analogous to removal of an impediment, such as a clattering noise or salt upon the tongue, which hinders the soul's departure. The latter are apparently considered to be in the category of *segulot,* i.e., non-natural and not proximately causal in nature, whereas drugs and medications are in the realm of rationally explainable, causally effective procedures. Alternatively, a distinction may be drawn between the state of *gesisah,* during which time the patient must be treated, and the actual moment of departure of the soul from the body, at which time man should not intervene.

It cannot be overemphasized that even the earlier-cited permissive authorities sanction acts of omission only when the patient is in a state of *gesisah.* At any earlier stage withholding of treatment is tantamount to euthanasia. What are the criteria indicative of the onset of this state? Rema defines this state as being that of the patient who "brings up a secretion in his throat on account of the narrowing of his chest."[12] Of course, if the condition is reversible there is an obligation to heal. When the condition of *gesisah* is irreversible there is no obligation to continue treatment and, according to some authorities, even a prohibition against prolonging the life of the moribund patient.

Rema's description, while a necessary criterion of *gesisah,* is certainly not a sufficient one. Were the patient to present this symptom but in the opinion of medical practitioners be capable of survival, he would clearly not be considered a *goses* and all usual obligations would remain in force. Moreover, the physiological criteria of *gesisah* must be spelled out with care. It is surely clear that a patient whose life may be prolonged for weeks and even months is not yet moribund; the actual death process has not yet started to commence and hence the patient is not a *goses.* The halakhic provisions governing care of a *goses* may most emphatically not be applied to all who are terminally ill.

It appears that any patient who may reasonably be deemed capable of potential survival for a period of seventy-two hours cannot be considered a *goses.* If the patient is capable of surviving this length of time, the death process cannot be deemed to have commenced. It would appear that Halakhah assumes axiomatically that the death process or the "act of dying" cannot be longer than seventy-two hours in duration. This is evidenced by the ruling that one must commence to observe the laws of mourning three days after a relative has been observed in a state of *gesisah.*[13] Some authorities even permit a wife to remarry in the absence of witnesses testifying to the actual death of the husband provided that testimony is forthcoming to the effect that her husband was observed in a state of *gesisah.* These authorities maintain that the testimony of witnesses with regard to *gesisah, ipso facto,* constitutes legal proof of a state of widowhood commencing three days following the onset of *gesisah.*

It appears that this state is not determined by a patient's ability to survive for this period solely by natural means unaided by drugs or medication. The implication is that a *goses* is one who cannot, under any circumstances, be maintained alive for a period of seventy-two hours. Testimony with regard to the existence of a state of *gesisah* as conclusive evidence of impending death implies that the state is not only irreversible but also not prolongable even by artificial means. Otherwise there would exist a legal suspicion that life may have been prolonged artificially by means of extraordinary medical treatment. The obvious conclusion to be drawn is that if it is medically feasible to prolong life, the patient is indeed not a *goses* and, therefore, in such instances there is a concomitant obligation to preserve the life of the patient as long as possible.

It follows that a specific physiological condition may or may not correspond to a state of *gesisah* depending upon the state of medical knowledge of the day. When medical care is of no avail and the patient manifesting the symptoms described by Rema is expected to expire within seventy-two hours, he is deemed to be in the process of "dying." When, however, medication can prolong life, such medicine, in effect, delays the onset of the death process. Accordingly, the patient who receives medical treatment enabling him to survive for a period of three days or more is not yet in the process of "dying." It follows, therefore, that those responsible for his care are not relieved of their duty to minister to his needs and to postpone the onset of death by means of medical treatment.

The aggressiveness with which Judaism teaches that life must be preserved is not at all incompatible with the awareness that the human condition is such that there are circumstances in which man would prefer death to life. The Gemara, *Ketubot* 104a, reports that Rabbi Judah the Prince, redactor of the Mishnah, was afflicted by what appears to have been an incurable and debilitating intestinal disorder. He had a female servant who is depicted in rabbinic writings as a woman of exemplary piety and moral character. This woman is reported to have prayed for his death. On the basis of this narrative, the thirteenth-century authority, Rabbenu Nissim of Gerondi, in his commentary on *Nedarim* 40a, states that it is permissible, and even praiseworthy, to pray for the death of a patient who is gravely ill and in extreme pain. He chides those who are remiss in discharging the obligation of visiting the sick, remarking of such an individual ". . . not only does he not aid [the patient] in living but even when [the patient] would [derive] benefit from death, even that small benefit [prayer for his demise] he does not bestow upon him."

Although man must persist in his effort to prolong life, he may, nevertheless, express human needs and concerns through the medium of prayer. There is no contradiction whatsoever between acting upon an existing obligation and pleading to be relieved of further responsibility. Man may beseech God to relieve him from divinely imposed obligations when they appear to exceed human endurance. But the ultimate decision is God's, and God's alone. There are times when God's answer to prayer is in the negative. But this, too, is an answer.

Contemporary rabbinic writers point out that even after Rabbi Judah's servant expressed her feelings and conveyed information regarding her master's pain and discomfort to his disciples, they not only declined to join her in prayer for his decease but did not desist from praying for prolongation of his life.[14]

There is one responsum in particular which deals with the question of prayer for termination of suffering through death, but which has important implications for decision-making in general. R. Chaim Palaggi, *Chikekei Lev,* I, *Yoreh De'ah,* no. 50, accepts the view of Rabbenu Nissim but expresses an important *caveat.* According to this authority, only totally disinterested parties may, by even so innocuous a method as prayer, take any action which may lead to a premature termination of life. Husband, children, family, and those charged with the care of the patient, according to R. Palaggi, may not pray for death. The considerations underlying this reservation are twofold in nature: (1) Those who are emotionally involved, if they are permitted even such non-physical methods of intervention as prayer, may be prompted to perform an overt act which would have the effect of shortening life and thus be tantamount to euthanasia. (2) Precisely because of their closeness to the situation, they are psychologically incapable of reaching a detached, dispassionate, and objective decision in which considerations of patient benefit are the sole controlling motives. The human psyche is such that the intrusion of emotional involvement and subjective interest preclude a totally objective and disinterested decision.

Decisions that available therapeutic methods shall not be employed because they are hazardous or of insufficiently demonstrated efficacy, or a decision that the patient is already in a state of *gesisah,* are also subject to unconscious bias because of the inability of the family and physician totally to transcend their personal and emotional involvement with the patient. It must, therefore, be stressed that Jewish scholars have long insisted that the pertinent facts be placed before a qualified rabbinic authority for adjudication on a case-by-case basis.

NOTES

1. *Orach Chaim* 329:4.
2. See J. Hamberger, *Real Encyclopaedia für Bibel und Talmud,* Supplement, II (Leipzig, 1901), p. 37; H. J. Zimmels, *Magicians, Theologians and Doctors* (London, 1952), p. 172, note 72.
3. *Yoreh De'ah* 339:1.
4. *Loc. cit.*
5. *Shabbat* 151b and *Semachot* 1:4.
6. See R. Eli'ezer Waldenberg, *Tzitz Eli'ezer,* XIII, no. 87. See also R. Natah Ze'ev Friedman, *Ha-Torah ve-ha-Medinah,* V–VI (5713–5714), 229; and R. Iser Y. Unterman, *Torah she-be-al Peh,* XI (5729), 14.
7. Cf. however, R. Isaac Liebes, *Teshuvot Bet Avi,* II, No. 153, p. 113. There may be room for an argument in support of withholding treatment in face of intractable pain so severe that the patient would willingly expend an entire fortune in return for its alleviation; cf. R. Abraham I. Kook, *Mishpat Kohen,* no. 144, sec. 17; and R. Moshe Feinstein, *Iggrot Mosheh, Yoreh De'ah,* II, no. 174, p. 294. See also *Shitah Mekubetzet, Ketubot* 33b, s.v. *u-be-kuntresin* and *Tiferet Yisrael, Yoma, Bo'az* 8:3.
8. *Tzitz Eli'ezer,* IX, no. 47, sec. 5.
9. *Ethics of the Fathers* 4:22.
10. *Yoreh De'ah* 339:1.
11. *Teshuvot Bet Ya'akov,* no. 59; *Iggrot Mosheh, Yoreh De'ah,* II, no. 174. Cf. also R. Moses Isserles, *Darkei Mosheh, Yoreh De'ah* 339.

However, *Shevut Ya'akov,* I, no. 13; *Bi'ur Halakhah, Orach Chaim* 329:2; and R. Eliezer Waldenberg, *Ramat Rachel,* no. 29, see no prohibition against prolonging the life of a *goses;* the latter two authorities view prolongation by means of accepted medical treatment as obligatory.

12. *Even ha-Ezer* 121:7 and *Choshen Mishpat* 211:2. See also the commentaries of Rambam and *Tosefot Yom Tov, Erukhin* 1:3.

13. *Yoreh De'ah* 339:2. See also *Derishah, Tur, Yoreh De'ah* 339:5, and *Teshuvot Bet Avi,* II, no. 153, p. 209.

14. *Ramat Rachel,* no. 5, and *Tzitz Eli'ezer,* IX, no. 47.

25

Time of Death

The formulation of a definition of death is in reality an attempt to arrive at an understanding of the very essence of human life. A living person is more than a mere organism. When endowed with a certain indefinable component, the organism is a vibrant human being; when that component is lost, what remains is nothing more than a corpse. The act of pronouncing a patient dead entails legal and moral ramifications of the highest significance.

The definition of death has serious medical, legal, moral and theological significance. Formulation of such a definition and the delineation of the precise moment at which death occurs is, in actuality, an endeavor to arrive at an understanding of the very essence of human life and of the nature of what it is which is lost at the time of death. Thus, theological considerations are of paramount importance.

For this reason much of the current debate concerning the determination of death misses the mark. A definition of death cannot be derived from medical facts or scientific investigation alone. The physician is eminently qualified to describe the physiological state which he observes. But he can do no more than report his clinical observations. Whether the patient meeting any description or set of descriptions is alive or dead is not, strictly speaking, a medical question. The physician may be called upon to determine whether medical science can or cannot be of further aid in restoring vital functions, but the physician possesses no esoteric information which will enlighten others with regard to the precise moment at which the moribund patient slips into death. Whether a human organism in any given physiological state is to be treated as a living person or as a corpse is an ethical, religious question and not a medical one. Accordingly, advances in medical science and technology have no effect upon Jewish teaching with regard to the establishment of time of death.

Until fairly recently man could do very little when afflicted by serious illness and hence was powerless in face of the ravages of nature and could only proclaim with resignation: "The Lord hath given, the Lord hath taken, may the name of the Lord be blessed" (Job 1:21). In recent times many have come to feel that since doctors and scientists have succeeded in prolonging life through the application of human intellect and scientific technology, it is fitting and proper that those selfsame individuals should be the arbiters of whether the quality of such life is worth preserving and, hence, of whether they may withhold their gift in a given situation. The argument acquires at least a measure of cogency when the decision to terminate life is reached for a purportedly higher purpose, e.g., transplantation of organs from a moribund person to a patient who may have chances for greater viability. The new dictum appears to be: "Science hath given, science hath taken, may the cause of science be blessed."

Nevertheless, from the perspective of classical Jewish ethics, any proposal for redefinition of the time of death which would have the effect of declaring a person to be deceased while any of the vital functions is yet present must be viewed as a threat to the very sanctity of human life. It is axiomatic that society has no moral right to sacrifice the life of one human being for the sake of another. No matter how laudable efforts to salvage organs for life-saving transplants may be, the snuffing out of the life of one person in the process of saving another is tantamount to murder.

Death as a concept, as distinct from a physiological state, is most frequently associated with the separation of the soul from the body. Indeed, the colloquial Hebrew phrase frequently employed as a synonym for death is *yetziat neshamah,* literally, "departure of the soul." Nevertheless, while departure of the soul from the body may constitute the essence of death, this phenomenon does not lend itself to direct empirical observation. Accordingly, other criteria must be sought which may serve as reliable indicators that this phenomenon has already occurred. The attempt to formulate a definition of death is thus really an attempt to identify the physiological criteria which serve as the symptomatic indications that the soul has departed from the body.

Common law and, until recently, all legal systems based upon that tradition defined death as "total stoppage of the circulation of the blood and a cessation of the animal and vital functions consequent thereupon, such as respiration, pulsation, etc."[1]

This definition of death is entirely consistent with the Jewish point of view and, indeed, was probably influenced by Jewish teaching. The talmudic discussion, which serves as the primary source for establishing the criteria of death in Jewish law (*Yoma* 85a), indicates that death may be assumed to coincide with cessation of respiration. The Gemara cites the verse "all in whose nostrils is the breath of the spirit of life" (Genesis 7:22) as indicating that life is present as long as respiratory activity persists. Indeed, the Sages understood this verse as indicating that the soul departs through the nostrils; the soul, in taking leave of the body, simultaneously causes respiration to cease and death to occur. The Midrash[2] notes that the first person described in the Bible as having been afflicted by sickness is Jacob and remarks that prior to the time of Jacob sickness was unknown. Jacob's illness was an answer to his prayer for prior indication of impending death in order that he might make a testament before dying. Before the days of Jacob, according to the Midrash, a person simply sneezed and expired without any other indication whatsoever that death was about to overtake him. In presenting the details concerning the creation of Adam, the Torah states, "and He blew into his nostrils the soul of life" (Genesis 2:6). The soul is thus described as having entered the body through the nostrils. According to the Midrash, the soul departs through the same aperture by which it entered. Since before the days of Jacob sneezing was indicative of the termination of life, the Midrash indicates that, now, upon sneezing one should give thanks for the privilege of remaining alive. Thus there arose the practice that we voice a wish, "To health!" or "God bless you!" upon hearing another person sneeze.[3]

Although the Gemara speaks of examination of the nostrils

as the most reliable criterion of death, rabbinic commentators indicate that cardiac activity is crucial in determining whether death has occurred. Cessation of respiration was employed as an operative definition of death only because, under ordinary circumstances, absence of breathing indicates that the heart has also stopped beating. This is clearly indicated by Rashi's choice of language in his comment upon the Gemara's discussion. In explaining the statement that it is not sufficient to examine the chest area to determine that the heart is not beating but that it is also necessary to examine the nose for possible breathing, Rashi comments, "At times life is not evident at the heart but is evident at the nose." It is readily understandable that a feeble heartbeat may not be audible or otherwise perceivable in a weakened patient (particularly before the invention of the stethoscope) since the rib cage and layers of tissue intervene between the heart itself and the outer skin.[4] Respiration is more easily detectable, and, therefore, Jewish law insists upon examination of the nostrils. However, in a situation in which life is not evident at the nose, for whatever reason, but *is* evident at the heart, cardiac activity is, in itself, sufficient to indicate that the patient is alive. Indeed, a renowned authority, Rabbi Zevi Ashkenazi, *Chakham Zevi,* no. 77, states definitively that the absence of cardiac activity is the crucial criterion of death and that respiration is simply an indicator of the presence of a heartbeat, for "there can be no respiration unless there is life in the heart." Thus, the renowned rabbinic authority, Rabbi Moses Sofer definitively declared that the patient may not be pronounced dead unless, in addition to total absence of respiration, the patient also "lies as an inanimate stone *and* there is no pulse whatsoever."[5] Pulsation is, of course, a direct demonstration of the presence of a heartbeat.

A clear understanding of this definition is necessary in light of life-support techniques available in the contemporary practice of medicine. Until recent times, life-sustaining machinery was not available. Accordingly, there was little reason to debate the precise moment at which death occurred since all relevant clinical signs of death tended to appear virtually simultaneously. At present this is no longer the case.

The most dramatic development in this area is the use of the respirator. This machine enables a patient no longer capable of spontaneous respiration to acquire life-supporting oxygen. The apparatus operates by forcing air into the lungs at set intervals. Oxygen is absorbed by the alvioli within the lungs and enters the bloodstream. Unabsorbed gases are forced out as the lung relaxes and contracts. The process which simulates breathing is quite literally an artificial form of respiration. It is also possible to attach a respirator to a person who has already died and to cause the lung to be artificially inflated and deflated. This does not mean that the person is alive. In terms of Jewish law, it is not necessary, or even permitted, to intebate a corpse. It is spontaneous respiration, as distinct from artificial respiration, which serves as a criterion of life.

Yet patients maintained on artificial respiration are very much alive. The indicator and cause of life is ongoing cardiac activity. It must be emphasized that the heart of a patient sustained on a respirator beats in an entirely normal and natural manner. The heartbeat is spontaneous. The respirator merely "breathes" for the patient; it does not cause his heart to beat artificially. The function of a respirator is precisely the same as that of the iron lung machine used to sustain polio victims incapable of independent respiration. There can be no doubt that iron lung patients, who are fully conscious and capable of engaging in many meaningful activities, are alive. Similarly, a patient maintained on a respirator must be considered to be alive even if he is in a coma, since the comatose state is not synonymous with death. Physicians who advocate a policy which would permit them to pronounce such a patient dead do so on the basis of an entirely different criterion of death, viz., "brain death," a criterion which is not acceptable from the point of view of Jewish law.

The respirator should not be confused with a heart-lung machine, which does perform a dual function. A heart-lung machine pumps blood and causes it to course through the body without the assistance of a normal, beating heart. This apparatus, which can sustain life for only a very limited period of time, is commonly used in conjunction with open-heart surgery, but is not medically appropriate for use as a life-sustaining mechanism in an otherwise terminal patient. Thus, a patient sustained on a respirator must be deemed to be alive by virtue of the presence of spontaneous cardiac activity.

Moreover, even minimal respiratory capacity is, *per se,* a sufficient criterion of life, even though utilization of a respirator is necessary to provide an adequate intake of oxygen. Accordingly, a respirator may not be removed lest this act itself hasten the demise of the patient.

It must also be stressed that only the *irreversible* cessation of respiratory and cardiac activity constitutes death. A patient who has experienced heart failure but who may be resuscitated is not yet dead. Were this not the case, it would lead to the conclusion that a patient undergoing open-heart surgery is actually dead during the period of time in which his cardiac and respiratory functions are taken over by an artificial apparatus. Even more absurd would be the inescapable inference that a doctor who resuscitates a patient has resurrected the dead! It is thus obvious that only irreversible cessation of respiratory and cardiac activity constitute the criteria of death.[6] It follows, of course, that Sabbath laws and other halakhic restrictions are suspended both on behalf of a patient on a respirator and on behalf of a patient for whom there is even the faintest hope of successful resuscitation.

As previously cited, Rabbi Moses Sofer adds a third criterion to the two previously discussed, viz., that the patient lie as an inanimate stone, i.e., total absence of all movement. This position is readily deducible from the comment of Rashi, *Yoma* 85a, who, in his explanation of the stated requirement for an examination of the nostrils, remarks that such examination is to be made if the person is "like a corpse which does not move its limbs." The clear implication is that, in the presence of such movement, the patient is deemed to be alive on the basis of manifestation of this vital sign alone.

Other authorities have stated that life may be present even in the absence of these perceivable criteria. Thus, if residual vital forces are in any way manifest, e.g., electrical activity in the heart as evidenced by means of an electrocardiogram or brain waves as recorded by an electroencephalogram, the patient must be deemed to be alive on the basis of such criteria alone.[7] Thus the earlier definition of death as "cessation of the animal and vital functions . . . such as respiration, pulsation, etc.," accurately reflects Jewish teaching even in the inclusion of the term "etc."!

Although in theory cessation of respiration and cardiac activity are the determining criteria in establishing that death has occurred, in practice this principle is considerably modified so that absence of these vital signs is not sufficient to establish that death has occurred. Halakhah provides that the Sabbath may be violated in order to save the life of an unborn fetus. Therefore the *Shulchan Arukh* states that if a woman dies in childbirth on the Sabbath, a knife may be brought through a public domain in order to make an incision into the uterus for the purpose of removing the fetus. However, Rema, in a gloss to this ruling, indicates that this provision, while theoretically valid, is inoperative in practice. Rema declares that, quite apart from the question of desecration of the Sabbath, it is forbidden to perform a post-mortem cesarean in order to save the fetus, on weekdays as well as on the Sabbath, because we are not competent to determine the moment of maternal death with exactitude.

Since it is forbidden to so much as move a limb of a moribund person lest this hasten his death, there can be no question of an incision into the womb until death has been established with absolute certainty. In view of the fact that by the time that the death of the mother can be conclusively determined the fetus is no longer viable, this procedure would be purposeless and consequently would constitute an unwarranted violation of the corpse.

The principle enunciated by Rema is that what may appear to be cessation of respiratory and cardiac activity cannot be accepted as an absolute criterion of death. Our lack of competence is due to an inability to distinguish between death and a fainting spell or swoon. In the latter cases respiratory activity does occur although respiration may be so minimal that it cannot be perceived.

In stating that we are incompetent to determine the moment of death with precision and cannot apply the criterion of respiration with reliability, Rema does not spell out clinical signs which may be accepted as conclusive. Nor does he indicate how much time must elapse following apparent cessation of respiration before the patient may be pronounced dead. There is some discrepancy in the writings of later authors with regard to establishing such a time period. A contemporary authority,

R. Yechiel Michal Tucatzinsky, *Gesher ha-Chaim,* I, chap. 3, p. 48, records that the practice in Jerusalem is not to remove the body from the deathbed for a period of twenty minutes following the presumed time of death. Earlier, R. Shalom Gagin, *Teshuvot Yismach Lev, Yoreh De'ah,* no. 9, stated that the custom in Jerusalem is to wait a period of one half-hour. Rabbi Gagin further noted that our incompetence to determine the time of death with precision should not necessitate a delay of "more than half an hour or at the most an hour" for final pronouncement of death.

A contemporary scholar[8] has argued that, in light of the clinical aids now available to the physician, the considerations which previously necessitated this waiting period are no longer operative. Rema's declaration that the ruling of the *Shulchan Arukh* is not followed in practice is based upon the fear that a fainting spell or swoon may be misdiagnosed as death. In many cases the possibility of such errors can be eliminated by use of a sphygmomanometer to determine that no blood pressure can be detected in conjunction with an electrocardiogram to ascertain that all cardiac activity has ceased. Accordingly, there is strong reason to advocate that, under such circumstances, the original ruling of the *Shulchan Arukh* now be followed in practice.

This suggestion should not be construed as an abrogation of Rema's ruling, since many authorities recognize that Rema's statement is based upon empirical considerations and admits to exceptions. For example, R. Ya'akov Reischer, *Shevut Ya'akov,* I, nos. 1 and 13, in discussing the bizarre case of a pregnant woman who had tragically been decapitated, sales unequivocally that the physician who had the presence of mind to incise the abdomen immediately in order to remove the fetus need have no pangs of conscience since, in this instance, the mother's prior death is established beyond cavil. Similarly, it may be argued, Rema's statement should not be viewed as normative under changed circumstances which enable medical science to determine whether death has already occurred. This argument is cogent in view of the fact that Rema himself remarks that it had become necessary to disregard the earlier authoritative decision of the *Shulchan Arukh* solely because of a lack of medical expertise. Granted that with the use of clinical aids one can establish conclusively that all cardiac activity has ceased, the contention that no further waiting period is needed is borne out by *Chakham Zevi's* previously cited statement, "There can be no respiration unless there is life in the heart."

In recent years there has been a concerted effort to modify the traditionally accepted criteria of death. The motivation is a twofold one: (1) to make organs available for transplantation before such organs become irreversibly damaged; (2) to eliminate the financial and emotional expense of sustaining the life of patients for whom medical science holds out no hope of recovery. The various proposals which have been offered center around differing forms of "brain death." The term "brain death," although it has attained wide currency, is a misnomer since the clinical criteria employed do not serve to establish the fact that the brain has been destroyed but rather are indicative of a dysfunction which has occurred within a limited part of the brain.

The most widely propounded proposal for a new definition of death is that of the Ad Hoc Committee of the Harvard Medical School. The recommended criteria of the Ad Hoc Committee are: (1) lack of response to external stimuli or need; (2) absence of movement or breathing as observed by physicians over a period of at least one hour; (3) absence of elicitable reflexes; and (4) a flat or isoelectric electroencephalogram. According to this definition, death is equated, not with destruction of the brain or even of a part of the brain, but with the loss of the body's integrating capacities as signified by the activity of the central nervous system. Indeed, the chairman of the Ad Hoc Committee candidly stated that the criteria offered are not a definition of death at all but constitute a definition of irreversible coma.[9] It is quite obvious that this definition of death is unacceptable from the point of view of Jewish law.

It is of more than cursory interest to note that in an earlier age Jews were subjected to bitter scorn for demanding immediate burial following manifestation of clinical signs of death. During the mid-nineteenth century various civil jurisdictions promulgated ordinances against precipitous burial. State authorities demanded a delay of as long as seventy-two hours following manifestation of clinical signs of death before permitting burial. Since Jewish law forbids such delay, rabbinic authorities of the day felt constrained to voice vigorous opposition. Moses Mendelssohn and other prominent figures of the Enlightenment urged a reconsideration of the Jewish position which they considered to be archaic and barbaric. During that period the halakhic definition of death was considered too liberal; at present it is deemed too conservative. The immutability of Jewish teaching regarding the definition of the time of death was affirmed in forceful terms by Rabbi Moses Sofer, who declared, "These are the clinical symptoms of death which have been transmitted to us from the time that the nation of God became a holy people. All the forces in the world . . . will not cause us to move from the position of our holy Torah."

Rejection of "brain death" as an acceptable criterion of death is entirely compatible with recognition that decapitation does serve as an incontrovertible indication of death even if spasmatic muscular movements persist after the head is severed. The Mishnah, *Oholot* 1:6, states: "And likewise cattle and wild beasts . . . if their heads have been severed, they are unclean [as carcasses] even if they move convulsively like the tail of a newt [or lizard] that twitches spasmodically [after being cut off]." However, the currently proposed criteria differ significantly from decapitation as described in the Mishnah. Decapitation involves destruction of the entire brain. It might be argued with cogency that total cessation of circulation of blood to the brain will result in destruction of brain tissue. *Total* destruction of the brain might then be equated with decapitation, and the patient pronounced dead after total destruction has occurred.[10]

However, in point of fact, there is at present no clinical method of determining whether total destruction of brain tissue has occurred. Radioisotope techniques, when and if sufficiently refined, may be employed only to determine that perfusion of the brain has ceased. Cellular decay of the brain does indeed commence upon cessation of blood flow but requires an indeterminate period of time to become complete. Cessation of circulation to the brain cannot, in itself, be equated with total cellular destruction of the brain.

Moreover, radioisotope scanning techniques cannot, in their current state of refinement, be utilized in order to determine that even perfusion of the brain has totally ceased. Investigators responsible for the development of these techniques claim only that such methods may be used to indicate cessation of circulation to the cerebrum, which is the seat of the so-called higher functions of the human organism, and are careful to describe the phenomena which they report as "cerebral death."[11] These phenomena are entirely compatible with continued circulation and perfusion of the medulla and the brain stem. In fact, radioisotope techniques do not even demonstrate total cessation of circulation to the cerebrum; they indicate only that effective circulation has decreased below the level necessary to maintain its integrity. Even if scanning methods currently used are accurate, they do not indicate that all circulation to even a part of the brain, i.e., the cerebrum, has been interrupted, but only that the rate of flow is below that necessary to maintain viability. Thus, in a summary of findings which forms part of a recent study, these techniques are described as "indicative of significant circulatory *deficit* to the cerebrum."[12]

The Harvard criteria are even less satisfactory than blood-flow tests as halakhic criteria for establishing that cellular decay of the brain has taken place. The Harvard criteria serve to establish only the dysfunction of a limited part of the brain; they do not constitute evidence that even a portion of the brain has been destroyed. *Oholot* 1:6 can be cited only to substantiate an argument that destruction of the *entire* brain is tantamount to death.

NOTES

1. *Black's Law Dictionary,* 4th ed., 1968.
2. *Pirkei de-Rabbi Eli'ezer,* chap. 52; and *Yalkut Shim'oni, Lekh Lekha,* no. 72.
3. Cf. R. Baruch ha-Levi Epstein, *Torah Temimah,* Genesis 2:22.
4. *Teshuvot Chakham Zevi,* no. 77.
5. *Teshuvot Chatam Sofer, Yoreh De'ah,* no. 338.
6. See Rabbi Moshe Sternbuch, *Ba'ayot ha-Zman be-Hashkafat ha-Torah,* p. 69; and R. Eli'ezer Waldenberg, *Tzitz Eli'ezer,* no. 25, chap. 4, sec. 5.
7. Rabbi Moses Feinstein, *Iggrot Mosheh, Yoreh De'ah,* II, no. 146.
8. Dr. Jacob Levy, *Ha-Ma'ayan,* Tammuz 5731.
9. Henry K. Beecher, "A Definition of Irreversible Coma," *Journal of the American Medical Association,* vol. 205, no. 6, pp. 337–340.

10. For an analysis of a statement by R. Moshe Feinstein regarding time of death, see J. David Bleich, "Neurological Criteria of Death and Time of Death Statutes," *Jewish Bioethics,* ed. Fred Rosner and J. David Bleich (New York, 1979), pp. 303–316. See also R. Aaron Soloveichik, "The Halakhic Definition of Death," ibid., pp. 296–302.

11. See P. Braunstein *et al.,* "A Simple Bedside Evaluation for Cerebral Death," *American Journal of Roentegenology, Radium Therapy and Nuclear Medicine,* vol. CXVIII, no. 4, August 1973, pp. 757–767, and Julius Korein *et al.,* "Radioisotopic Bolus Technique as a Test to Detect Circulatory Deficit Associated with Cerebral Death," *Circulation,* vol. 51, May 1975, pp. 924–939.

12. Korein, p. 924.

26

Suicide

Suicide is equated with murder in Jewish law. The prohibition against suicide is derived from Genesis 9:5, which is rendered as "your blood from your [own] persons shall I require," i.e., God declares that He will punish the person who spills his own blood. The punishment destined for the suicide is of necessity a heavenly one to be meted out in the afterlife. There is a well-known aphorism to the effect that a suicide has no share in the World-to-Come. This adage is not to be found in any of the extant talmudic writings, although R. Jacob Emden reports that he found such a reading in one edition of the Talmud, Tractate *Semachot.*[1] It is not surprising that such punishment is assumed, since the act of suicide by its very nature signifies with finality that the perpetrator lacks concern for divine commandments.

Jewish teaching with regard to suicide is rooted in the concept that man does not enjoy proprietary rights with regard to his body or his life. God, as the Author of life, entrusts the human body to the stewardship of man for preservation and safekeeping but retains to Himself title to life. Accordingly, man's life is not his to dispose of at will. A thirteenth-century scholar, Rabbi Judah the Pious, *Sefer Chasidim,* no. 675, extends this concept to the preservation of health in asserting that a person who neglects his health has violated the stewardship which has been imposed upon him.

In some respects suicide is an even graver sin than murder. A person who commits murder may regret his deed and be sincerely repentant. The suicide, however, by nature of the finality of his action, precludes the possibility of repentance. Furthermore, death itself is a form of expiation of sin. However, since the act of suicide is itself a cardinal transgression, it cannot be an atonement for sin. Moreover, the act of suicide, unlike murder, constitutes a denial of divine mastery over mankind and is tantamount to denial of divine creation of man.[2] In addition, willful suicide is a denial of the immortality of the soul. A person who commits suicide as a means of avoiding pain or humiliation, were he to acknowledge the existence of a life after death, could not fail to recognize that the punishment to which he is destined in the World-to-Come will be even more painful and humiliating.

Some authorities permit martyrdom by means of suicide, at least in some circumstances. A person must sacrifice his life rather than transgress one of the three cardinal sins, viz., idolatry, murder, and some forms of sexual immorality. Martyrdom is also required in face of coercion with regard to lesser infractions during periods of forced apostasy or when such an infraction is demanded as a public act which may be construed as signifying a renunciation of Jewish teaching in whole or in part. Some authorities permit a person who fears that he will not be able to withstand torture designed to make him submit to a demand of this nature to take his life by his own hand in order to prevent an act which constitutes a profanation of the Divine Name. It is for this reason that, at times, entire communities committed suicide rather than face forced apostasy.[3] Under such circumstances suicide, according to these authorities, is not a violation of divine will but rather an act of sanctification of the Divine Name.

The usual signs of honor and respect accorded the deceased are omitted in the case of a suicide because the body is deemed to have lost its status as a "container" of sanctity and holiness. The corpse is buried outside the gate of the cemetery or at least at a distance of eight cubits from other graves.

Although in theory Jewish law treats suicides very harshly, in practice these provisions are seldom applied. A person is innocent until proven guilty. This principle applies to an apparent suicide no less than to other transgressors. A coroner's verdict of death by suicide carries no weight in Jewish law. The Talmud, *Semachot* 2:2, declares that if a person had been observed ascending a roof and later was seen falling from the building, or if a person is found dead with a sword by his side or even in his hand, he is not presumed to have taken his own life. Some authorities extend this provision by adding that even if the person declared he was about to kill himself, or left a note to that effect, the word is not to be associated with the deed because, particularly under stress, people frequently make frivolous or unmindful statements. A person is adjudged a suicide only on the basis of incontrovertible evidence.

Some authorities indicate that the treatment prescribed in Jewish law for suicide is to be applied only if death follows immediately upon the suicidal action, e.g., suicide by means of a self-inflicted mortal wound which causes instantaneous death. If, however, there is a lapse of time between the suicidal act and demise, it should be assumed that the person in question regretted his action and that his contrition removes him from the category of those to whom these regulations apply. Moreover, if there is reason to believe that the suicide was emotionally distraught or high-strung, and as a result was not in full possession of his faculties, he is not deemed a willful suicide "for it is remote that a person should perform a disgraceful act such as this with a clear mind."[4] It must, however, be emphasized that the compassion expressed in the applicable provisions of Jewish law with regard to the burial and mourning of a suicide are provisions which apply only after the fact. No person may aid or abet a suicide or even provide counsel which would imply that the act of suicide may be condoned even in extreme circumstances.

One further leniency is recorded in a responsum of R. Moses Sofer, *Teshuvot Chatam Sofer, Yoreh De'ah,* no. 326. This authority indicates that the honor of the family whose members are innocent of any misdeed must be taken into account. It would be unjust to expose them to shame and ignominy in instances when this can be avoided. Therefore, he rules that if attendant circumstances are such that it is possible for people to be led to think that the person was not a suicide, or that extenuating circumstances render the laws pertaining to suicide inapplicable, the deceased should not be treated as a suicide even though, in point of fact, it is known with certainty that he does fall into this category. Thus, the law of suicide is set aside to preserve the honor of the family when (1) there is a family whose members would be adversely affected and (2) treatment of the deceased as a non-suicide is credible in the eyes of the public.

NOTES

1. See also *Midrash Shochar Tov,* Psalms 120, which states, "Doeg, who killed himself, has no share in the World-to-Come." See also *Torah Temimah,* Genesis 9:5, and *Tosefet Berakhah,* Genesis 9:5.
2. Rabbi Yechiel Michal Tucatzinsky, *Gesher ha-Chaim,* I, no. 25.
3. See *Da'at Zekenim me-Ba'alei ha-Tosafot,* Genesis 9:5.
4. *Arukh ha-Shulchan* 345:5.

27

Autopsy

Judaism requires that a corpse be accorded every sign of respect. Eating, drinking or frivolous behavior in the presence of the deceased are forbidden as not in keeping with the dignity which is due the human body. Physical assault upon the human body is, *a fortiori,* forbidden in death as well as in life. It is in light of these factors that Judaism forbids post-mortem pathological examinations which involve anatomical dissection.

The obligation to honor the dead and the prohibition against violation of the corpse are predicated upon the biblical directive: "And if there be in a man a sin deserving of death, and he be put to death, and you hang him on a tree; his body shall not remain all night upon the tree, but you shall surely bury him the same day; for he that is hanged is a reproach to God" (Deuteronomy 21:22–23). The direct reference of this statement is to a person convicted of a capital transgression. The body of even a common criminal who is put to death for his malevolent deed is inviolate subsequent to his execution.

Since man is created in the "image of God," the human body must be treated with respect; failure to do so is deemed to be "a reproach to God." The Sages, commenting upon this verse, present an allegorical interpretation of this concept.[1] They liken the situation to that of twin brothers, one of whom becomes a king and the other a bandit. The bandit is executed in punishment for his crime. Were his corpse allowed to remain hanging, passers-by who happened to gaze upon it would believe that it was the king who had been hanged and treated in so ignominious a manner. To be certain, Judaism emphatically rejects any anthropomorphic description of the Deity.

Nevertheless, this allegory serves to underscore the fact that the human soul is sanctified by God and hence its earthly habitat, the human body, shares in this sanctity. For this reason the Torah forbids any sign of disrespect and demands immediate burial as befitting a sacred vessel.

There is, however, some question with regard to the precise nature of the prohibition against dissection of the corpse. According to one line of reasoning, the prohibition against desecration of the dead is rooted in the individual's divinely bestowed right to the physical integrity of his body in death no less than in life. Violation of the corpse is then primarily a crime against man, akin to theft and physical assault, and only secondarily a sin against God. This view was adopted by the nineteenth-century German scholar, R. Ya'akov Ettlinger.[2] On the basis of this line of reasoning, R. Ettlinger felt compelled to reach a most stringent conclusion, namely, that since dissection of the dead is a crime against man, it cannot be sanctioned even for purposes of saving a human life. According to Jewish law, appropriation of property belonging to another person for purposes of saving a life is certainly warranted. It is, however, justifiable only on condition that proper financial compensation be made subsequently. R. Ettlinger argues that no restitution for physical desecration of a corpse is possible and, hence, one dare not violate the corpse. Moreover, he contends, the situation is not entirely analogous to unauthorized use of material possessions. A living person whose property is appropriated for such use is himself under obligation to save human life. The deceased, on the contrary, are "free of the commandments" and are not bound by any such obligation. Other scholars, however, engaged in extensive argumentation in order to demonstrate that autopsy for purposes of preservation of life may indeed be sanctioned.

On the other hand, R. Ya'akov Ettlinger's position does admit of a leniency. Since dissection of the dead is a violation of laws "between man and man," any person is at liberty to forgo personal privileges and forgive infractions of his rights. Hence, R. Ettlinger rules that a body may be dissected if the deceased himself gave permission while yet alive. However, relatives or next-of-kin do not have the prerogative of relinquishing rights enjoyed by the deceased.

This line of reasoning was employed by subsequent authorities in sanctioning autopsies which may be of help in treating progeny of the deceased afflicted by a genetic disease or the like even in the absence of express permission on the part of the deceased. Understandably, it is assumed that a parent would be willing to suffer any necessary indignity in order to preserve the life of his child. The argument that it is an honor for the deceased to have his corpse utilized for the sake of advancement of medical knowledge in general was expressly rejected by the eminent eighteenth-century scholar, R. Ezekiel Landau of Prague, whose responsum[3] (which will be discussed in more detail later) is regarded as the definitive formulation of Jewish teaching with regard to autopsies.

Other authorities, however, disagreeing with R. Ettlinger, explain the nature of the prohibition against desecration of the dead in a totally different manner. These scholars are of the opinion that the infraction is a violation against God rather than against man. Man is created *be-tzelem Elokim,* in the image of God; an assault upon the body of the deceased thus constitutes an act of disrespect toward God. The body is a vessel which, when alive, contains within it a sacred soul; as such, the body itself is an object of holiness. The effect of this line of reasoning is to deny to man the authority freely to give permission for the desecration of his corpse. On the other hand, according to this analysis, it is clear that sanction is readily forthcoming if preservation of human life is at stake. The consensus of opinion among contemporary rabbinic decisors is to sanction autopsies for purposes of preserving life but to forbid autopsies for other purposes even if the deceased has granted consent prior to his death.

R. Landau indicates that a post-mortem anatomical examination may be permitted for one other purpose as well, viz., in the case of a murder victim when such examination is necessary in order that the murderer be convicted and executed. To allow the murderer to remain unpunished is a dishonor to the homicide victim. Hence, argues R. Landau, whatever is necessary to bring the culprit to justice constitutes an honor to the deceased. Thus, in such limited circumstances, the autopsy procedure, while it is a violation of the corpse, is designed to enhance the dignity of the deceased and is accordingly permissible.[4]

The selfsame considerations apply to cadaver transplants. Organs may be transplanted if such transplantation is designed to cure or alleviate a life-threatening condition from which the recipient suffers. For reasons which will be explained below, removal of organs for transplant purposes is permissible only if there is a patient awaiting a transplant. Organs may not be removed for storage in an organ bank for use at some future time.

In recent years a Uniform Donor Act has been enacted in all fifty states and in the District of Columbia. This act makes provisions for a person to make an anatomical gift of his body, in whole or in part, after death has occurred. Donor cards, formulated in conformity with the provisions of this act, now appear on the reverse side of drivers' licenses in approximately forty states. Holders of such licenses are encouraged to sign the donor card in order to make their organs available after death for transplantation purposes. The text of this document, however, contains extremely broad language in terms of authorization for post-mortem procedures. It provides that organs and parts of the body may be utilized not only for transplantation but also for purposes of "therapy, medical research or education." This document is thus an authorization for unrestricted use and study of organs after death even if there exists no immediate threat to the life of another person. Furthermore, this document makes no provision for ultimate return of organs and tissue for purposes of burial. Jews cannot sign such a blanket authorization without violating their religious principles. Nor, even if such a document is signed, is it permissible to perform such post-mortem procedures, since it is the accepted view that man lacks the authority to dispose of his body even after death. Consent of next-of-kin for otherwise illicit procedures is also meaningless insofar as Jewish law is concerned. Since a person cannot freely dispose of his body, it follows, *a fortiori,* that his heirs have no authority to do so either.

In terms of normative Halakhah, the prevailing view is that an autopsy may be performed if it is envisioned that the information gained thereby will contribute to the preservation of life. In this regard, dissection of the dead, although it involves violation of a biblical prohibition, is no different from any other act which is otherwise forbidden but is sanctioned in face of danger. The issue requiring clarification is a precise formulation of the type of danger regarded as sufficiently grave to warrant suspension of biblical injunctions.

R. Ezekiel Landau, in his celebrated responsum on this subject, states definitively that the suspension of any prohibition is permissible only for the benefit of an already endangered patient, or, in rabbinic terminology, a *choleh le-faneinu* (lit. "a patient in front of us"). The concept of a *choleh le-faneinu* is, roughly speaking, the halakhic equivalent of the legal concept of "a clear and *present* danger." Laws may be suspended for purposes of saving an endangered life but not in anticipation of a hypothetical eventuality. R. Landau demonstrates the cogency of this position by means of a *reductio ad absurdum:* If laws and regulations are to be suspended in anticipation of some future benefit to a person as yet not endangered, no prohibition would be meaningful. Cooking on the Sabbath, for example, would then be justified on the grounds that perhaps someone might take sick and require hot food. There is virtually no act which might not, in some unanticipated way, contribute to the preservation of life. For violation of halakhic restriction to be justified, there must be a discernible connection between the contemplated act and elimination of an existing danger.

Accordingly, an autopsy cannot be performed in the vague hope that, serendipitously, some potentially life-saving knowledge may be gained in the process of post-mortem examination. However, an autopsy would, for example, be warranted in the case of a patient who has died after receiving an experimental drug or drug combination which had been administered to a group of patients. Post-mortem examination to ascertain possible toxicity foreboding potential harm to other patients on the same course of treatment or for purposes of obtaining information concerning the therapeutic efficacy of the drug or drug combination would be warranted according to Halakhah when such information is deemed to be essential in the treatment of other patients already suffering from the same illness. Of course, in any given situation the matter should be submitted to a competent rabbinic authority for a ruling on a case-by-case basis.

It is for this reason that organs cannot be removed after death for storage in an organ bank. Removal of an organ is warranted only if there is a *choleh le-faneinu,* i.e., a patient who will benefit directly thereby, but not for storage in anticipation that, at some future time, the organ may be utilized for a life-saving purpose.

The prohibition against post-mortem examination is suspended only to the extent necessary for obtaining information required for treatment of other patients similarly afflicted. The usual autopsy involves an incision extending over the entire length of the abdominal and thoracic cavities and examination of all internal organs. Post-mortem examinations routinely include the opening of the cranium and examination of the brain as well. These procedures cannot be countenanced when—as is usually the case—all pertinent potentially life-saving information may be acquired by means of a much more limited incision and examination of only those organs or areas crucial for obtaining this information. Organs may not be removed if they can be examined *in situ.* All organs and body fluids must be returned for burial.

The autopsy dilemma has frequently been compounded by the fact that even when a limited autopsy is warranted in accordance with Jewish law, Halakhah imposes various restrictions both with regard to the extent of the autopsy and the manner in which it must be performed. Pathologists, accustomed to performing post-mortems on a routine basis, are frequently unaware of these restrictions. Well-intentioned medical personnel are often not cognizant of the religious sensitivities and practices of the patient and family. The consent forms which are in general use are blanket in nature and legally give the hospital staff virtual *carte blanche* in conducting these procedures.

When an autopsy is sanctioned in accordance with the provisions of Jewish law, the pathologist should be requested to state in precise clinical terms the information he seeks, specifying the area to be incised and the organs to be examined in obtaining such information. The authorization signed by the next-of-kin should limit the extent of the post-mortem procedure to that which is absolutely necessary in order to secure pertinent, potentially life-saving information of immediate applicability. Granting limited consent morally and legally obligates the pathologist to respect the directives of the next-of-kin. The next-of-kin should specify in writing the limitations placed upon the autopsy procedure and, in addition, secure written assurance that all organs, tissues, and fluids will be returned for burial as required by Jewish law. A form designed for this purpose will be found on p. 187 of this volume.

Some authorities have ruled that post-mortem peritoneoscopy, a procedure which does not require an incision but merely the introduction of an electrical instrument into the body, is permitted since the procedure involves no assault upon the body. Removal of a blood sample after death by means of needle puncture, as well as post-mortem needle biopsies, are also permitted by some on the basis of a similar rationale.[5]

A new method of post-mortem examination has recently been developed by a team of physicians headed by Dr. Samuel Schorr, professor of diagnostic radiology at the Sackler School of Medicine, Tel Aviv University. This method requires no invasion of the corpse other than by means of a simple needle injection and would be sanctioned by those authorities who permit removal of blood and post-mortem needle biopsies.

This method involves injection of a contrast fluid which can be seen clearly on X-ray film. The fluid is injected into one of the bones of the body shortly after death and leaves no discernible mark upon the body. The contrast fluid spreads rapidly through the blood vessels, allowing for clear X-ray pictures of blood vessels and through them the vital organs such as the liver and kidneys. Tumors, ruptures of these organs, and blood clots are clearly visible upon X-ray examination. It is anticipated that with further development and refinement a high degree of diagnostic accuracy will be achieved.

NOTES

1. *Sanhedrin* 46b.
2. *Binyan Zion,* nos. 170–171.
3. *Noda be-Yehudah, Yoreh De'ah,* II, no 210.
4. Cf. *Teshuvot Me'orot Natan, Yoreh De'ah,* no. 79.
5. *Iggrot Mosheh, Yoreh De'ah,* II, no. 151.

Afterword

Judaism calls upon man to accept not only gladness and joy but also pain and suffering as emanating from God. The Sages of the Talmud ruled that a person is obliged to pronounce a blessing in praise of God upon experiencing misfortune just as he must praise God upon experiencing good fortune. R. Akiva declared, " 'You shall not make with Me gods of silver' (Exodus 20:20). [This is to be understood as meaning] 'Do not conduct yourself with Me as other nations [do with their gods].' They respect them when fortune smiles upon them and curse them when misfortune strikes. Of you God demands, 'When I bring you good, give thanks; and when I visit evil upon you, give thanks.' " (*Mekhilta* 10:2).

Perhaps the most difficult sacrifice which may be demanded of man is not that he surrender his life, but that he surrender his autonomy. A life can be sacrificed but once, but the will must be surrendered over and over again. Contemporary man often finds his natural inclinations to be at variance with the revealed word of God. When such conflict arises a person may readily acknowledge that, although the struggle may be herculean, sensual desires must at times be sublimated for the sake of spiritual aspirations. But when man experiences what he perceives to be the voice of conscience speaking in a language which is inconsonant with that of religious authority his dilemma is far more acute. Judaism calls upon him to acknowledge that perceived moral intuitions are not always veridical. Man's will, even when he perceives it to be directed by the loftiest and most altruistic of motives, must bow to superior divine wisdom.

A curious phenomenon besets Jewish life today. A generation of Jews born, reared, and educated on these shores has grown to maturity. Qualitatively and quantitatively, members of this generation are observant of the tenets of Judaism far beyond the fond dreams of their mentors. Yet, all too many of those who bear their distinctiveness with pride fail to appreciate the uniqueness of the Jewish *Weltanschauung.* A person meticulous in observance of the Sabbath may be indistinguishable from his non-observant and even from his non-Jewish colleagues in his professional conduct. A person exceedingly careful that no morsel of forbidden food pass between his lips may fail to exercise the same discrimination with regard to the advice he dispenses in his office or business. This happens only because people tend to assimilate attitudes prevalent in the cultural milieu in which they find themselves. Jews who pattern their lives upon Torah teaching are known as orthodox rather than as orthoprax. The Torah demands not only correct practices but correct attitudes. One should not anticipate the attitudinal foci of Judaism to be at one with those of the dominant culture. The Jew whose opinions with regard to social issues and societal concerns are influenced by the Op-Ed page of the daily newspaper rather than by sacred writ perforce becomes the victim of a curious religious schizophrenia. His ritual observance may be exemplary, but his attitudes and actions in the multifarious aspects of daily life may actually be antithetical to Torah values.

Judaism is an all-pervasive discipline of life. Its standards are unique. Its values are not the product of human inquiry but of divine revelation. Its moral norms are theocentric rather than homocentric. Little wonder, then, that the Jewish response to the moral dilemmas of our age is so often in striking discord with contemporary mores. Nowhere is this more pronounced than in bioethics.

The topics discussed in this book currently engage the attention of countless academicians and policy-makers. It should be quite evident that Judaism has specific teachings with regard to each of these areas of inquiry. At times those teachings are at variance with conventionally accepted wisdom. But there is one strand which runs throughout and which accounts for virtually all areas of divergence. The many detailed laws of Jewish bioethics are expressions of the supreme value which Judaism places upon the precious gift of life.

Human life—and the human body—are precious because they are the gifts of the Creator who demands of us that we cherish them. Man's duties with regard to his body and his life flow from an awareness that, in truth, body and life are not his to defile or to destroy, but to sanctify and to safeguard until reclaimed by the Creator. In fulfilling the sacred obligations of this stewardship man must put his faith and trust in God and seek strength in the awareness that God, to whom all things are possible, bestows the fortitude necessary to discharge faithfully the awesome responsibilities which He imposes upon His creatures. In discharging these duties, man eloquently bears witness that "*Ha-neshamah lakh ve-ha-guf pa'alakh*"—not only is the soul Yours, but the body is Your handiwork as well.

Appendix I

The Jewish Patient's Bill of Rights

The American Hospital Association has adopted a "Patient's Bill of Rights" to clarify what a patient may expect from a hospital administration. Since an observant Jewish patient has additional specific needs, Agudath Israel of America has prepared this "Jewish Patient's Bill of Rights," to assist hospital administrators in properly caring for such patients. We know that hospitals, eager to offer the most effective healing facilities to all of their patients, will welcome this clarification of Jewish needs.

1. The Jewish patient can be admitted to the hospital in an emergency on the Sabbath or a Festival, by making an oral statement of authorization suitably witnessed. No patient may be forced to sign an admission form in violation of religious scruples.
2. The Jewish patient has the right to be served Kosher food of proper quality, quantity, and variety to assure meeting his nutritional needs.
3. The Jewish patient has the right to medical attention, and to defer any advanced payment that may normally be required until the close of the Sabbath or Festival.
4. The Jewish patient has the right to engage in observance of Jewish ritual where not medically counterindicated. This includes prayer, provisions for Sabbath candles, Chanukah Menorah, Kosher-prepared wine, Esrog and Lulav, Matzoh, Megillah reading, and Shofar, where appropriate and possible. The hospital should recognize the psychological value of these activities in the same spirit as

recreational and other amenities that are offered to the patient.

5. The Jewish patient has the right to refuse out-patient appointments scheduled for the Sabbath and Festivals, the eve of such days, or fast days. This refusal should not prejudice the patient's right to a suitable alternative appointment.
6. The Jewish patient has the right to consult with his own spiritual advisor—or allow family to do the same when patient is incapable of doing so—before deciding on procedures involving abortion, sterilization, prostate surgery, contraception, artificial insemination, circumcision, euthanasia, autopsy, withdrawal of life-supporting therapy or appliances, hazardous procedures, or any other procedure posing religious questions. The name of the family rabbi should be entered on hospital admission cards, as a matter of routine, so he may be called upon to serve as consultant when religious problems arise.
7. The Jewish patient has the right to expect the hospital to consider consultation with a spiritual advisor as professional guidance, which can assist immeasurably in the treatment of the patient as a complete entity. The rabbi should be considered an integral part of the healing team.
8. The Jewish patient has the right to psychiatric, psychological, genetic, sex and other counseling by individuals attuned to patterns of behavior which are the norm among observant Jews. The medical team should welcome the participation and advice of the patient's spiritual advisor.
9. The Jewish patient has the right to request such considerations as those listed above for visitors whose presence is deemed supportive of the patient's health and well-being.

To the Patient:
We are confident that a polite but forceful request for any or all of these rights will be honored by hospital administrators. While these rights may not be legally binding, they are certainly ethically and morally binding. Efforts are now being made to secure endorsement of these rights by hospitals across the

country. Showing this statement to attending personnel will help you in stating your claim for the right to all that the medical profession has to offer you, without compromising your religious convictions.

Prepared by
Agudath Israel of America

Appendix II

The Bereaved Jew's Bill of Rights

For centuries, the organized Jewish community—the *kehilla*—dealt with every special circumstance in the life cycle, *simcha* and tragedy. Thus, from the time a person died until after the mourning period, the *Chevra Kadisha* (burial society) responded to the needs of both the deceased and the survivors—as delineated by *halacha,* tradition, and local custom. It was deemed an honor for a man or woman to be selected to join their respective *Chevra* (for men or women), and once appointed, the member discharged his/her duty with the utmost fidelity to the letter and spirit of the law.

As is well known, much in the way of communal life was lost in the flow of immigration from Europe to America. In many cases, various organizations, *Landsmannschaften* and fraternal societies had their own *Chevra Kadisha.* In other cases, especially in smaller towns, the creation of a new *Chevra Kadisha* was assumed by the community. Sometimes the American *Chevros* discharged their duties with a fidelity that matched their European counterparts, but in other cases, unfortunately, control of the *Chevra* fell into the hands of people with little regard for *halacha,* who viewed the burial society as a means for profiteering.

The person in charge—bearing the title of *Gabbai, Hospitaler* or Chairman of the Cemetery Committee—was always on call. When a death occurred, he immediately took charge of all arrangements, from *shmira* (guarding the body) and *tahara* (ritual cleansing before burial) to burial.

The eulogies customarily took place in front of the home of the deceased or on the steps of the *shul* he attended. The undertaker supplied the coffin, hearse and cars, if requested.

The organization generally had established a standard price with the undertaker, for which he furnished a specific type of coffin (with or without nails, depending on custom), the hearse, and other transportation for mourners. With the exception of the information needed for the death certificate, the family of the deceased was spared from making any arrangements and negotiating prices; all dealings were transacted by the *Gabbai, Hospitaler,* etc. who was also the sole contact with the cemetery.

As the more dedicated *Chevra* members passed from the scene, expensive funeral chapels proliferated. Funeral directors influenced the organizations to permit them to speak directly to the family, and under stress, shame them into buying a fancy casket—bearing fancy prices—in direct violation of Jewish law and tradition. Today, with the exception of funerals handled by the few dozen active Orthodox organizations, 98% of the burials are made in elaborate, expensive, wooden or even metal caskets, many with outer protective concrete vaults—totally contrary to Torah law. Other practices contrary to *halacha,* such as embalming, "open coffins," and unattended burials—have also been instituted, either under the pretext that they are legal requirements, or by exerting strong emotional pressures on the bereaved.

Regrettably, many responsible organizations and *Chevros* are going out of existence, and their function is being taken over by funeral directors. In some cases, the state takes over a *Chevra* when it is informed of its pending dissolution. To protect the members' burial rights, many of the old *Chevras* have merged so as to maintain some semblance of Orthodoxy in their activities, without interference from the younger generation, which to a great extent does not care about such matters. It is essential that we do whatever we can to restore halachic integrity to this crucial and sensitive phase of human existence.

INTRODUCTION

Just as strict adherence to Torah laws and practices apply in dealing with the living, so are they mandatory in dealing with the deceased. Thus, all events prior to and following a death are subject to the principles of the Jewish religion.

A death in the family generally besets the survivors with a numbness that makes it difficult for them to insist upon the strict adherence to halachic guidelines for respecting the dead. It is therefore most important that a competent authority—an Orthodox rabbi experienced in this field, or the head of the deceased's *Chevra Kadisha*—be contacted as early as possible in case of bereavement. His involvement in the funeral arrangements ensures that the deceased will be treated with dignity and care as defined by *halacha*.

This outline of "rights" is being issued as a service to the Jewish community with several purposes in mind. For one, the unaware individual should be alerted to some of the problems encountered in emergency situations, when no qualified authority is available. Well-intentioned managers of funeral homes can be poorly informed in regard to the requirements and sensibilities of the Jewish bereaved. For that matter, doctors and hospital personnel can at times also be unresponsive to Jewish needs. In addition, public authorities are often ignorant of religious Jewish funeral practices; legislation and regulations that limit traditional practices and customs are in violation of Freedom of Religion, and should be eliminated.

It is hoped that the increased awareness engendered by this Bill of Rights, coupled with the good intentions of all concerned, will serve to prevent and protect our brethren from unnecessary hurt and sorrow at the time of their bereavement.

THE SIGNS OF DEATH

There is unanimity among rabbinical authorities that the time of death is determined by the cessation of breathing and heartbeat. Absence of brain waves as recorded by an electroencephalograph, even when accompanied by absence of other vital signs, does not indicate death—all legislation to this effect notwithstanding. To the observant Jew, a declaration of death based upon neurological criteria is much more than a violation of his/her rights of Freedom of Religion. Under such circumstances, the patient is often still alive and treating him as though he were dead in regard to medical treatment and follow-up procedures CANNOT BE PERMITTED. Medical personnel MUST look for the classical signs of death before making a declaration of death.

TIME OF DEATH

It is important to know the precise time of death for the purpose of honoring the deceased's *yahrzeit* after the first year. The exact time of burial is significant for sitting *shiva*—the mourning period. It is also important that the decedent's doctor sign the death certificate quickly to facilitate burial without undue delay. Next of kin should record the full Hebrew name of the deceased and that of his/her father.

THE NEXT OF KIN

As soon as next of kin are notified of their relative's passing, they should immediately contact their rabbi or *Chevra Kadisha* for assistance and guidance on how to proceed. This will help ensure that preparation for burial as well as the interment itself are carried out in accordance with Jewish law. The above applies whether the death takes place at home, in a hospital, or while the person was on a distant trip abroad.

PRACTICES TO WHICH A JEWISH DECEASED MUST NEVER BE SUBJECTED

AUTOPSY AND REMOVAL OF ORGANS

Any alteration in a corpse, such as takes place during an autopsy or in the removal of an organ, is a desecration of the dead to be avoided in all normal circumstances. Where the life of another individual requires one of these procedures, an Orthodox rabbi must be consulted *before* the procedure takes place. Unfortunately, medical personnel often put undue pressure on next of kin to permit autopsies, imparting the impression that the law requires their performance, when it is not really so. NO CONSENT FORM SHOULD EVER BE SIGNED WITHOUT CONSULTING A RABBINICAL AUTHORITY.

Relatives of a person who died accidentally or as a result of suspected violence (circumstances that by civil law require postmortem examinations) are advised to contact their rabbi as soon as possible, to determine the halachic stand on the particular case. To reiterate: any *unjustified* alteration in a corpse is a desecration.

When postmortem examinations *are* justified, they must be limited; and after examination, the remains must be treated with respect and brought to burial. [A model limited consent form is included as Appendix III.] Bed linens and clothing that are stained with blood lost in death are to be secured from the hospital (or other such institution), for in certain cases they require burial with the deceased.

Limbs and organs removed from a person during his lifetime should preferably be buried. Those removed for any reason after death require burial. Under all circumstances a competent rabbi should be consulted as to the procedure.

EMBALMING

The embalming process, wherein the blood of the deceased is replaced by an embalming fluid, is strictly forbidden by Jewish law as a gross desecration of the body. Morticians who embalm the remains of a Jewish deceased person as a matter of course violate the religious sensibilities and rights of the deceased and the survivors. A rabbi should be consulted regarding procedures for the purpose of transportation.

CREMATION

Cremation of the remains of a Jewish person is a gross desecration strictly forbidden by Jewish law. It is an act that reflects a total negation of belief in *Techiyas Hameisim*—resurrection of the dead—which is a basic principle of faith. When a person mandates cremation of his remains, his ashes are not to be interred in a Jewish cemetery, and in many cases, the surviving family is not required to observe the usual mourning period.

COSMETIC PREPARATION AND VIEWING

Cosmetic treatment of the body of the deceased is forbidden. Public viewing of the body is considered an outrageous humiliation of the dead, in complete violation of the spirit and the letter of the *halacha.* By the same token, relatives are forbidden to embrace the deceased, or even touch him except when involved in preparation for interment.

DELAYED BURIAL

The body of the deceased must be buried as soon as possible, preferably on the day of passing. Exceptions can be made in unusual circumstances, but only upon the ruling of an Orthodox rabbi. Otherwise, every delay is an offense to the dead.

THE BURIAL PROCESS IN ACCORDANCE WITH JEWISH LAW

GUARDING THE BODY

Jewish law requires that a *shomer* lit.—"guard," should be with the body as much as possible from the time of death up to the time of burial; this includes accompanying the body whenever it is being transported. The *shomer* should preferably be an Orthodox Jew, personally committed to the belief that the body must not be subjected to any indignities, as defined by Jewish law. The importance of the *shomer's* assignment is such that he is exempt from carrying out any other religious responsibilities while on his watch. After the body has already been placed in a box or vault, there are various opinions on the matter.

RELEASE OF THE BODY

The next of kin is usually required to sign some sort of Authorization of Release Form. He must be alert to the prevalence of standard release forms that authorize the chapel to embalm and otherwise desecrate the body of the deceased. He should never sign a release form before reading it carefully. It is always advisable to enlist a rabbi's advice in this matter. Funeral homes that make use of such deceptive forms are guilty of consumer fraud and should be reported to local authorities.

TRANSFER OF THE BODY

In the absence of a *Chevra,* it is the responsibility of the funeral director to arrange for transfer of the body from the hospital, home, or morgue to the chapel and then to the cemetery; the next of kin should insist that a *shomer* accompany the body at all times. Sometimes the director will arrange for the *shomer.* An authority should be consulted as to the *shomer's* suitability.

PREPARATION OF THE BODY (TAHARA)

The *Tahara*—ritual cleansing of the body—is the only process involving the body of the deceased that is required by Jewish law. *Tahara* is properly performed by a *Chevra Kadisha*—sometimes an independent group associated with the community, in other cases in cooperation with the funeral chapel. To ensure that this intricate procedure is carried out with fidelity to tradition *by people of piety and reliability,* the suitability and expertise of the members of a *Chevra Kadisha* should be verified by an Orthodox rabbi.

CLOTHING THE BODY (TACHRICHIM)

The body is clothed in simple white burial shrouds, preferably made of linen. As in the case of the coffin, the simplest garment is mandated by Jewish law.

COFFIN

The body should be placed in a plain all-wooden casket, unadorned and unembellished in any way. Least expensive is almost by definition "kosher" in regard to the coffin. Coffins made of concrete, metal, and other such materials, as well as the use of linings, are expressly forbidden. The traditional coffin has one or several holes bored through a panel near or on the bottom.

THE FUNERAL SERVICES

The funeral is a religious service and thus should be under the complete guidance and direction of an Orthodox rabbi, with his presence and participation through the completion of burial.

The funeral parlor's primary concern is with providing a chapel with adequate provision for services in accordance with Orthodox tradition.

KRI'AH

Primary mourners (parents, siblings, spouse and children) must rend outer garments—usually at the time of the funeral service or the burial, but occasionally at some other time closer to the deceased's passing, depending upon *minhag* (custom) and other variables. The black "mourning ribbon" has no place in Jewish tradition.

BURIAL

The funeral procession should not be elaborate or ornate in any way. The contemporary use of decorative floral arrangements has no place in the Orthodox funeral.

While ideally, only observant Jews should be charged with opening the grave, it is often left to the cemetery administration, which assigns the task to professional cemetery workers. Care should be taken that the grave *not* be dug before the day of burial.

When a death occurs on a legal holiday, or on the previous day, the cemetery workers in New York State are required to open a grave providing that the cemetery office is informed by 9 AM of the holiday. A strike by cemetery workers should not be permitted to cause a delay in burial. If necessary, family, friends, and others are obligated to provide burial in as expeditious a manner as possible. To whatever extent possible, only observant Jews should lower the coffin and cover it with earth. The closing of the grave (that is, completely filling the cavity, above the level of its sides or at least to the depth of three handbreaths: 9″–12″) marks the formal completion of the burial, and the beginning of the period of mourning. It is an integral part of a procedure of religious significance. All earth removed from the excavation should be replaced on the grave.

The custom of holding a wake has no place in Jewish tradition, and only serves to dishonor the dead.

CONCLUSION

Proper observance of the dignity of the dead is a matter of great priority in Judaism. Next of kin who are able to carry out the burial of a loved one in a dignified manner can take comfort in the fact that they have accomplished a *gemilas chessed* (act of charity) to the deceased of the very highest order.

It is hoped that with time it will no longer be necessary to insist upon proper practices by funeral parlors and cemeteries. In the meantime, a polite but forceful insistence upon one's rights to adhere to one's religious dictates will ensure respectful treatment and proper burial of the deceased. A funeral director who proclaims that he "will not permit a rabbi/*Chevra* to interfere with my funeral" is acting unethically and should be overruled by responsible family members.

May *Klal Yisroel* and all its members be spared further sorrow, and may death be forever banished from the face of the earth.

Prepared by
Commission on Legislation
and Civic Action
Agudath Israel of America
Dr. Bernard Fryshman, Chairman

Appendix III

Authorization for Limited Autopsy

USE OF LIMITED CONSENT FORM

Judaism teaches that man is created in the image of God. Every dignity must be extended to the human body in death as in life. It is for this reason that the body must be regarded as inviolate. It is well known that, except in certain very limited circumstances, Jewish law does not sanction the performance of autopsies. It is, however, the consensus of rabbinic opinion that post-mortem examinations may be performed for the purpose of gaining specific information of benefit in the treatment of other patients already afflicted by a life-threatening disease. A case in point would be a person who has died after receiving an experimental drug or drug combination which had been administered to a group of patients. Post-mortem examination to ascertain possible toxicity foreboding potential harm to other patients on the same course of treatment or for purposes of obtaining information concerning the therapeutic efficacy of the drug or drug combination would be warranted according to Halakhah when such information is deemed to be essential in the treatment of other patients already suffering from the same illness.

The prohibition against post-mortem examination is suspended only to the extent necessary for obtaining information necessary for treatment of other patients similarly afflicted. The usual autopsy involves an incision extending over the entire length of the abdominal and thoracic cavities and examination of all internal organs. Post-mortem examinations routinely include the opening of the cranium and examination of the brain as well. These procedures cannot be countenanced when—as is usually the case—all pertinent potentially life-saving information may be acquired by means of a much more limited incision and examination of only those organs or areas crucial for obtaining this information. Organs may not be removed if they can be examined *in situ.* All organs and body fluids must be returned for burial.

The autopsy dilemma has frequently been compounded by the fact that even when a limited autopsy is warranted in accordance with Jewish law, Halakhah imposes various restrictions both with regard to the extent of the autopsy, and the manner in which it must be performed. Pathologists accustomed to performing post-mortems on a routine basis are frequently unaware of these restrictions. Well-intentioned medical personnel are often incognizant of the religious sensitivities and practices of the patient and family. The consent forms for obtaining permissions which are in general use are blanket in nature and legally give the hospital staff virtual *carte blanche* in conducting these procedures.

The attached form has been prepared by the author in consultation with a number of physicians and legal scholars. It is designed to provide for detailed specification of the nature and scope of the post-mortem examination for which permission is sought. This consent form requires the physician to state in precise clinical terms the information he seeks, to specify the area to be incised and the organs to be examined in obtaining such information. The authorization signed by the next of kin limits the extent of the post-mortem procedure to that which is absolutely necessary in order to secure pertinent, potentially life-saving information of immediate applicability. Use of the consent form morally and legally obligates the pathologist to respect the directives of the next of kin. It specifies the limitations placed upon the autopsy procedure and, in addition, assures that all organs, tissues and fluids will be returned for burial as required by Jewish law.

The form also specifies that the family may designate a representative to be present during the performance of the autopsy. Every effort should be made for either a rabbi or an observant physician to be in attendance. This will serve to assure that the proper procedures are followed scrupulously and that decorum consistent with the respect properly due the deceased is maintained.

It should be emphasized that this limited consent form is designed for use *only in conjunction with autopsies receiving rabbinic sanction.* A competent rabbinic authority must be consulted in *each individual case* before consent is given by the next of kin. The attached consent form serves to guarantee that, when a rabbinic authority has sanctioned an autopsy, such autopsy will, in fact, be carried out in conformity with the dictates of Halakhah.

To be completed in triplicate. One copy to be retained by person granting authorization for performance of autopsy.

....HOSPITAL

.... STREET

AUTHORIZATION FOR LIMITED AUTOPSY

Name of Deceased: .... Age at Death: ....

History No.: .... Date of Death: ....

....

The undersigned, being the husband ......wife ......next of kin ......of the deceased,

....and being charged by law with the duty of burial,

does hereby authorize .... HOSPITAL to perform a limited autopsy on the body of said deceased subject to such restrictions as set forth below:

These restrictions are mandated by the deep religious convictions of the deceased and of the undersigned whose faith prohibits post-mortem examinations when performed other than in the manner indicated. In consonance with these religious convictions this authorization is granted solely upon the prior representation that such autopsy and/or pathological study is absolutely necessary for the purpose of acquiring information essential for the treatment of other patients afflicted by a similar illness or disease and that there is strong expectation that such autopsy and/or pathological study will yield pertinent information of immediate and potentially life-saving value in treating other patients similarly afflicted.

Authorization is granted for performance of an autopsy and for pathological study limited to only the following organs or areas of the body: ....

....

and only to the extent necessary for the purposes of obtaining the following specific

information: ....

....

The incision is to be as limited as possible consistent with obtaining this information. Permission for an open procedure is not granted if a needle biopsy of limited incision with biopsy over a single organ or structure can yield this information. Organs are not to be removed from the body if an *in situ* examination proves to be sufficient for this purpose. Biopsy and/or removal of organs is to be limited to these organs the examination of which is necessary in order to yield the above specified information.

It is further stipulated that all organs, tissues and body fluids, including blood and other serous effusions, whether within the body cavities or without, will be preserved for burial save for such minute amounts which are deemed necessary for microbiological testing and/or preparation of microscopic slides. It is further stipulated that the body together with all organs, tissues and body fluids will be returned for burial

no later than .... a.m. .... p.m. on ...., ...
hour day date

It is also stipulated that in performance of such autopsy, care shall be taken to preserve the dignity of the deceased; the body shall be draped and only the area of biopsy or incision exposed; the demeanor of those performing the autopsy shall be respectful; and the autopsy shall be carried out with the same consideration of human dignity as is customary in surgical procedures.

The undersigned reserve the right to have a designated representative present during the performance of this autopsy.

Signed: ....Relationship to Deceased: ....

Witnessed by: ....Witnessed by: ....

Date of Authorization: ....Signed: ....M.D.
Member of Hospital Staff Obtaining Consent

Approved: ....General Manager

Bibliography

The interested reader may find information relating to Jewish law and medicine in the following works:

Abraham, A. S. *Medical Halachah for Everyone.* Jerusalem: Feldheim Publishing Co., 1980.

Bleich, J. David. *Contemporary Halakhic Problems.* New York: Ktav Publishing House, 1977.

Jakobovits, Immanuel. *Jewish Medical Ethics.* Revised edition. New York: Bloch Publishing Co., 1975.

Rosner, Fred. *Modern Medicine and Jewish Law.* New York: Yeshiva University Press, 1972.

———, and J. David Bleich, eds. *Jewish Bioethics.* New York: Hebrew Publishing Co., 1979.

אברהם, אברהם-ספר. **לב אברהם.** ב׳ כרכים. ירושלים תשל״ז-תשל״ח.

הרשלר, משה. **הלכה ורפואה.** ירושלים תש״מ.

ישר, הרב ברוך. **לרפואה שלמה: דיני רפואה לחולה לרופא ולמטפלים.** ירושלים, תשל״ג.

כפיר הרב א. **הלכות נתוחי חולים ומתים.** ירושלים, תשכ״ח.

נויבירט, הרב יהושע ישעיה. „דיני רפואה בשבת״, **סידור מנחת ירושלים,** נערך ע״י הרב י. א. דבורקס. ירושלים, תשל״ז. ע׳ 475 — 522.

נויבירט, הרב יהושע ישעיה. **מדריך הלכתי לאחיות בבתי חולים לשבת ולמועדים.** ירושלים, תשל״ו.

נויבירט, הרב יהושע ישעי׳ה. **שמירת שבת כהלכתה.** מהדורה חדשה, ירושלים, תשל״ט.

שטיינברג, אברהם. הלכות **רופאים ורפואה: על פי שו״ת ציץ אליעזר להגרא״י וולדינברג.** ירושלים תשל״ח.

שטרן, הרב מיכל. **הרפואה לאור ההלכה.** ירושלים תש״מ.

Indices

I. PASSAGES CITED

1. Bible

2. Talmud

II. NAMES AND SUBJECTS